CAMPAIGN • 255

# THE NAVAL BATTLES FOR GUADALCANAL 1942

Clash for supremacy in the Pacific

**MARK STILLE**          **ILLUSTRATED BY HOWARD GERRARD**

*Series editor Marcus Cowper*

First published in Great Britain in 2013 by Osprey Publishing,
Midland House, West Way, Botley, Oxford OX2 0PH, UK
43-01 21st Street, Suite 220B, Long Island City, NY 11101, USA
E-mail: info@ospreypublishing.com

A CIP catalog record for this book is available from the British Library.

ISBN: 978 1 78096 154 5
E-book ISBN: 978 1 78096 155 2
E-pub ISBN: 978 1 78096 156 9

Editorial by Ilios Publishing Ltd, Oxford, UK (www.iliospublishing.com)
Index by Fionbar Lyons
Typeset in Myriad Pro and Sabon
Maps by Bounford.com
Battlescene illustrations by Howard Gerrard
Originated by PDQ Media, Bungay, UK
Printed in China through Worldprint

13 14 15 16 17   10 9 8 7 6 5 4 3 2 1

## ACKNOWLEDGMENTS

The author is indebted to the staffs of the US Naval History and Heritage
Command and the Yamato Museum for their assistance in procuring the
photographs used in this title.

## ARTIST'S NOTE

Readers may care to note that the original paintings from which the color
plates in this book were prepared are available for private sale. The
Publishers retain all reproduction copyright whatsoever. All enquiries
should be addressed to:
Howard Gerrard, 11 Oaks Road, Tenterden, Kent, TN30 6RD
The Publishers regret that they can enter into no correspondence upon this
matter.

## THE WOODLAND TRUST

Osprey Publishing are supporting the Woodland Trust, the UK's leading
woodland conservation charity, by funding the dedication of trees.

# CONTENTS

# American and Japanese bases in the South Pacific

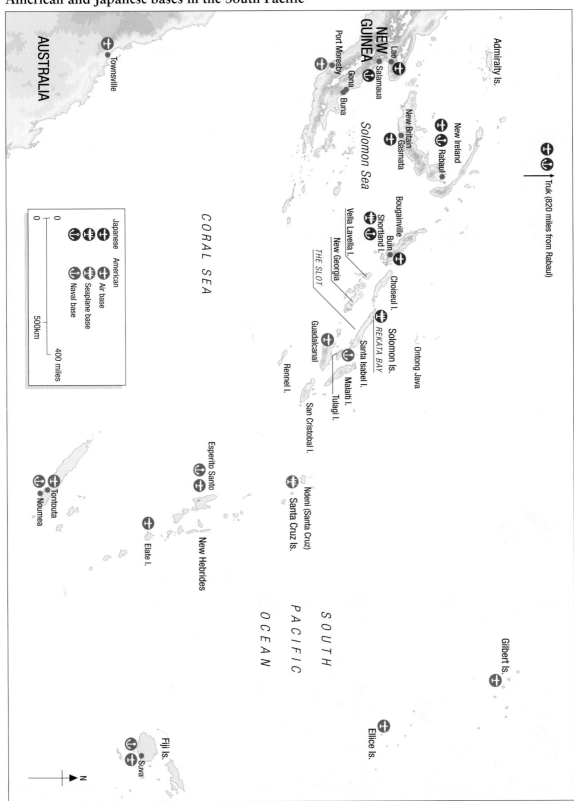

# INTRODUCTION

Neither the United States nor the Imperial Japanese Navy (IJN) thought that the decisive battle of the Pacific War would be fought over an obscure island located in the southern Solomon Islands. Nevertheless, for six months from August 1942 until early February 1943, both navies found themselves locked in the most sustained naval campaign of the Pacific War, centered on the island of Guadalcanal. This campaign included seven major battles. Two of these were fought between carriers, but the other five, all at night, pitted the surface forces of the two navies against each other in a series of vicious, often close-quarter battles. Ultimately, the campaign was decided by the possession of the airfield on Guadalcanal. The Americans were able successfully to keep the airfield open throughout the campaign, making it difficult and ultimately impossible for the Japanese to move sufficient ground forces to the island to dislodge the Americans. At the conclusion of the campaign, both navies had suffered heavy losses. These were easily replaced by America's growing wartime production, but, for the Japanese, the losses were crippling. Guadalcanal was the first stop on the long road to Tokyo.

## ORIGINS OF THE CAMPAIGN

Occupation of Guadalcanal was not envisioned in Japan's prewar expansion plans. In the First Operational Phase, the Imperial Army and Navy jointly agreed to occupy the Philippines, Malaya, the Dutch East Indies, Burma, and Rabaul. This went largely as planned. Rabaul, on the island of New Britain in the South Pacific, was occupied in January 1942. Rabaul possessed a large harbor and several airfields and was an ideal jumping-off location for further expansion in the area.

After the easy successes in seizing the First Operational Phase objectives (with the exception of the Philippines, which were not entirely occupied until May), the Japanese faced the question of where to advance next. As always, the availability of shipping was the primary limiting factor, though Japan's ground and naval forces were already being stretched. The goal of the Second Operational Phase was to provide strategic depth to Japan's defensive perimeter. In addition to the Aleutians and Midway, much of the anticipated future expansion would occur in the South Pacific. Eastern New Guinea, the Fijis, Samoa, and "strategic points in the Australian area" were all targeted. However, the Japanese could not agree on the validity of these objectives or the sequencing of the operations. Within the IJN, the commander of the

Combined Fleet, Fleet Admiral Yamamoto Isoroku and the Naval General Staff had very different priorities. Yamamoto wanted to move first into the Central Pacific with the goal of drawing the remaining units of the US Pacific Fleet into battle and destroying them. The Naval General Staff advocated an advance into the South Pacific to cut the sea lines of communications between the United States and Australia. For its part, the Imperial Army favored operations that required minimal numbers of ground forces. This ruled out an attack on Australia, but operations against smaller South Pacific islands remained possible.

Though the Naval General Staff was the organization responsible for the formulation of Japanese naval strategy, Yamamoto's views largely prevailed. Just as he had in the planning period before the Pearl Harbor operation, he used the threat of resignation to get his way. However, the decision reached in the first week of April was a compromise that called for an advance into both the South and Central Pacific in the span of two months. The first operation was set for May with the goal of seizing Port Moresby on New Guinea. Part of this operation was the occupation of Tulagi Island in the southern Solomons. Tulagi could be used as a seaplane base and was located some 20 miles north of Guadalcanal.

Japanese preparations for a major operation into the South Pacific did not escape the notice of the Americans. The Commander of the US Pacific Fleet, Admiral Chester Nimitz, dispatched two carrier groups to contest the Japanese advance. This resulted in the first carrier battle of the war in the Coral Sea on May 7–8, 1942, and the first strategic Japanese defeat of the war since the invasion of Port Moresby was halted. However, Tulagi was occupied according to plan on May 3, which gave the Japanese a foothold in the southern Solomons.

Another result of the Coral Sea battle was the fatal undermining of Yamamoto's clash with the American fleet in the Central Pacific. None of the three Japanese carriers committed to the Port Moresby operation was able to participate in the Midway operation in June. This significantly reduced Yamamoto's carrier advantage over Nimitz, and, combined with weak operational and tactical planning, resulted in a disaster for the IJN. All four of Yamamoto's fleet carriers committed to the operation were sunk. These losses blunted Japan's naval offensive capabilities. Following the Midway debacle, the Japanese made no attempt to maintain the initiative they had held since the beginning of the war. But the Japanese were not entirely passive. On June 13, they decided to build an airfield on Guadalcanal. Accordingly, on July 6, a 12-ship convoy arrived with two construction units to start work on the airfield, which was expected to be completed in August. Possession of an airfield on Guadalcanal would give the Japanese control over much of the South Pacific.

# THE AMERICAN RESPONSE

Admiral Ernest King, Commander-in-Chief US Fleet, had been focused on the South Pacific since the beginning of the war. He made the defense of the sea lines of communication to Australia a major priority. Even though overall American strategy called for the primary effort to be made in Europe, King did not think that meant he had to be totally passive in the Pacific. As early as March 1942, King admitted that he had no intention of remaining strictly defensive but envisioned an offensive up the Solomons to retake Rabaul. In the aftermath of the Midway victory, which removed the Japanese offensive threat in the Central Pacific, King moved quickly to grab the initiative and launch a limited offensive in the South Pacific.

Even with the prospect of gaining strategic surprise, King's limited offensive operation in the South Pacific was a very risky operation. After Midway, Yamamoto's Combined Fleet still outnumbered the Pacific Fleet in every combatant category except submarines. More importantly, the logistic foundation for major operations in the region was shaky. None of this deterred King. Shortly after the Japanese occupation of Tulagi on May 3, American planners were working on a plan to recapture it. The original date of the operation was set for August 1. After intelligence provided an assessment that Japanese construction troops were on Guadalcanal, the island was added as an objective on July 5.

The invasion force, centered on the 1st Marine Division, was quickly assembled. Delays in loading the Marines in Wellington, New Zealand, forced a delay in the landings until August 7. On July 22, the Marines departed en route to Guadalcanal. Escorting the invasion force was the bulk of the US Pacific Fleet, centered around three carriers. The first American counteroffensive of World War II was under way.

The Japanese conducted a major operation into the South Pacific in May 1942, which resulted in the battle of the Coral Sea. The Japanese suffered a strategic defeat, losing the light carrier *Shoho*, shown here on fire. The Japanese did successfully occupy Tulagi Island in the southern Solomons, setting up the Guadalcanal campaign. (Naval History and Heritage Command, 80-G-17046)

# CHRONOLOGY

| | |
|---|---|
| **August 7** | Americans land on Guadalcanal. |
| **August 9** | Battle of Savo Island: four Allied heavy cruisers sunk for no Japanese losses. |
| **August 20** | First American aircraft arrive at Henderson Field. |
| **August 21** | Battle of the Tenaru River: first Japanese attempt to seize Henderson Field is repulsed. |
| **August 24–25** | Battle of the Eastern Solomons: Japanese attempt to destroy American fleet and to run a small reinforcement convoy to Guadalcanal is defeated. |
| **September 12–14** | Battle of the Bloody Ridge: second Japanese ground attack on Henderson Field repulsed. |
| **September 15** | Carrier *Wasp* sunk by Japanese submarine attack. |
| **October 11–12** | Battle of Cape Esperance: first Japanese defeat in a night battle during the war. Japanese lose one heavy cruiser and one destroyer. |
| **October 14** | Two Japanese battleships bombard and temporarily neutralize Henderson Field. |
| **October 15** | Two Japanese heavy cruisers bombard Henderson Field. |
| **October 15** | Japanese reinforcement convoy arrives on Guadalcanal; three of six transports sunk by air attack but 4,500 troops land. |
| **October 15–16** | Two Japanese heavy cruisers bombard Henderson Field. |
| **October 18** | Ghormley relieved by Halsey. |
| **October 24–25** | Japanese ground attack on Henderson Field fails. |

| | |
|---|---|
| October 26 | Battle of Santa Cruz: Japanese carrier force gains a tactical victory against its American counterpart, but carrier *Enterprise* escapes to play a key future role in the campaign. |
| November 13 | First Naval Battle of Guadalcanal: Americans suffer heavy losses but turn back Japanese attempt to bombard Henderson Field with battleships. |
| November 13–14 | Two Japanese heavy cruisers bombard Henderson Field but fail to neutralize it. |
| November 14 | American aircraft sink one heavy cruiser and six of 11 transports in a convoy bound for Guadalcanal. |
| November 14–15 | Second Naval Battle of Guadalcanal: Halsey commits two battleships to defeat another Japanese attempt to conduct a battleship bombardment of Henderson Field. One Japanese battleship is sunk. |
| November 15 | Last four Japanese transports are sunk. Yamamoto's final attempt to recapture Guadalcanal is defeated. |
| November 29–30 | Battle of Tassafaronga: Japanese lose a single destroyer but sink one heavy cruiser and heavily damage three more. |
| December 31 | Japanese finalize plans to evacuate Guadalcanal. |
| January 29–30 | Battle of Rennell Island results in the sinking of one American heavy cruiser by Japanese torpedo aircraft. |
| February 1 | First evacuation run to Guadalcanal by 20 Japanese destroyers picks up 4,935 personnel; one destroyer is lost to mines. |
| February 4 | Second evacuation run with 20 destroyers picks up another 3,921 personnel against no opposition. |
| February 7 | Last evacuation run by 18 destroyers picks up final 1,972 personnel. |
| February 9 | Organized Japanese resistance on Guadalcanal ends. |

# OPPOSING COMMANDERS

## JAPANESE COMMANDERS

The Commander of the Combined Fleet during the Guadalcanal campaign was Admiral **Yamamoto Isoroku**. Despite the disaster at Midway, Yamamoto's reputation was still high. Reputation aside, Yamamoto was a mediocre strategist. His greatest victory, the Pearl Harbor operation, was an act of strategic folly which severely undermined any hope the Japanese had of securing a negotiated peace with the United States. His fatal compromise with the Naval General Staff in April set the stage for defeat in both the Coral Sea and Midway.

Yamamoto made Midway his personal battle, and in the aftermath of that smashing defeat he was caught off balance by the American offensive into the Solomons. In response, Yamamoto was slow to respond. Though the Combined Fleet still possessed a margin of strength over the Pacific Fleet, Yamamoto always seemed one step behind during the Guadalcanal campaign. Not until late August did he assemble a force to retake the island. The first attempt was ill-conceived and achieved neither of Yamamoto's goals of destroying the American fleet or landing reinforcements on the island. The fact that the entire operation was mounted to move a reinforcement convoy with only 1,500 troops (when the Americans already had over 10,000 troops on the island) shows how muddled Japanese operational planning was.

At no point in the campaign did Yamamoto bring his superior force to bear. The result was to turn the battle into a grinding battle of attrition which the Japanese could not afford. In mid-September, the Americans were down to a single operational carrier. Though Yamamoto had four, he did not seize this chance. In October, Yamamoto stepped up efforts to regain the island. At one point, he even threatened to bring his flagship (the superbattleship *Yamato*) alongside Guadalcanal. This was exactly what was needed – total commitment. In the end, he did commit battleships to bombard Guadalcanal's airfield, but Yamamoto always seemed more concerned with maintaining the Imperial Fleet for a decisive battle than fighting the battle he had at hand.

In late October 1942, Yamamoto fought a major carrier battle with the Americans off Guadalcanal. It was his greatest victory over the American Navy, but he was unable and unwilling to follow up. Convinced that three American carriers had been sunk (only one had been, with another escaping), he withdrew part of his carrier force from the campaign, leaving the burden on the Japanese surface forces. When the Guadalcanal campaign came to a climax in November, Yamamoto attempted to bombard the airfield again with battleships. Even now, he did not commit all available forces. The Americans did, and it proved enough to turn back the Japanese. Yamamoto never realized that Guadalcanal was the decisive battle he had been seeking. In the November battles, the Japanese were not so much outfought as undermined by timid leadership. Yamamoto oversaw the evacuation of the remaining Japanese garrison from the island in February 1943. In April, an aircraft he was riding in was shot down and he was killed over the northern Solomons. Ironically, the American fighters responsible came from Guadalcanal.

Vice Admiral Mikawa Gunichi commanded the Rabaul-based 8th Fleet throughout the campaign. He gave a superb performance at the opening battle of Savo Island, but then failed to exploit his victory. (Naval History and Heritage Command, NH 63697)

The commander of Japanese naval forces in the Solomons was Vice Admiral **Mikawa Gunichi**. He was a 1910 graduate from the IJN academy at Eta Jima and placed third in his class of 149. He was identified early in his career as an officer of promise, and held several important overseas and staff positions. In his fleet positions, he became an expert in navigation and commanded heavy cruisers *Aoba* and *Chokai* and battleship *Kirishima*. Mikawa was promoted to flag rank in December 1936. Following command of cruiser and battleship squadrons, he was promoted to vice admiral in November 1940. When war came, he was commander of Sentai (Squadron) 3 composed of the four Kongo-class battleships and was assigned as the commander of the screen of the IJN's carrier force.

In July 1942, Mikawa was placed in command of the new 8th Fleet (also known as the Outer Seas Force) based at Rabaul and responsible for operations in the Solomons. This was seen as a backwater command, as was shown by the fact that his fleet consisted of mainly older units. Even so, these units, led by Mikawa, rendered the US Navy its worst defeat of the war at the battle of Savo Island. He continued in command of the 8th Fleet throughout the campaign and personally led the cruiser bombardment of Henderson Field on the night of November 13–14, 1942. He was charged with the responsibility of moving Imperial Army troops to Guadalcanal and keeping them supplied. He was largely successful in this effort until late in the campaign, despite the fact that he did not have command of the air and thus had to conduct all movements at night, which forced the use of destroyers as transports, a mission for which they were ill suited. He was relieved as commander of the 8th Fleet in April 1943.

Because of his failure to attack the American transport fleet after his victory at Savo Island, Mikawa was one of the most controversial Japanese naval leaders of the war. It is significant that his failure to attack the transports was not seen by the Japanese as a fatal blunder at the time. In destroying the enemy's naval strength, he was simply adhering to the classic Japanese precepts of naval power. The inability to seize the unique opportunity after Savo Island was a manifestation of the inflexibility of Japanese naval leadership in general. Mikawa performed well for the remainder of the Guadalcanal campaign and, following Japan's defeat at Guadalcanal, he continued to hold important commands.

Vice Admiral Kondo Nobutake was the loser of the Second Naval Battle of Guadalcanal, where his tentative tactics allowed a smaller American force to thwart his bombardment of Henderson Field. (Naval History and Heritage Command, NH 63696)

Rear Admiral Tanaka was a veteran of many actions off Guadalcanal, including his signal victory in the battle of Tassafaronga in November. This performance gained him the respect of his American counterparts, but he was criticized by some Japanese figures for not providing leadership and leaving the conduct of the battle to his subordinates. (Naval History and Heritage Command, NH 63429)

An often-overlooked IJN command figure was Vice Admiral **Kondo Nobutake.** He graduated from Eta Jima in 1907 and spent his entire career on surface ships until being promoted to flag in 1933. As a vice admiral at the start of the war he was the commander of the 2nd Fleet, which was charged with the important task of covering the invasion of Malaya and the Dutch East Indies. Kondo conducted this mission successfully, and then commanded the invasion force in the abortive attack on Midway. At the start of the Guadalcanal campaign, he was Yamamoto's principal seagoing commander. In this capacity, he performed well at Eastern Solomons and Santa Cruz. When the battleships were committed to the actions around the island, Kondo was drawn in as well. He was in command of the Japanese naval forces at the Second Naval Battle of Guadalcanal in November, but his poor tactics resulted in defeat and he lost a battleship in the process. Despite this, he was treated gently and was later promoted to admiral but never held another seagoing command. Kondo was by all accounts a capable officer, and was known for his aggressiveness.

Rear Admiral **Goto Aritomo** was a 1910 graduate of Eta Jima. He spent his entire career in surface ships until being promoted to flag in November 1939. When the war began, he was commander of Sentai 6, a division of the four oldest heavy cruisers in the IJN in September 1941. During the battle of Coral Sea, he commanded the Main Body and lost light carrier *Shoho* to air attack. He was present at Savo Island where his well-drilled cruisers provided the backbone of the victorious Japanese force. On October 12, he led the Japanese force at the battle of Cape Esperance. His total disregard for even the possibility of an American attempt to challenge him in a night battle led to his force being surprised and defeated. He was killed on his flagship by American shellfire.

One of the most prominent Japanese naval figures of the Guadalcanal campaign was Rear Admiral **Tanaka Razio.** He graduated from Eta Jima in 1913. His career included tours on destroyers, battleships and even as a commander of a submarine squadron. He began the war as commanding officer of the 2nd Destroyer Squadron. This unit saw action during the invasion of the Dutch East Indies and the battle of Midway. Tanaka saw action in every major engagement of the Guadalcanal campaign and his name has been linked with the destroyer reinforcement and resupply runs to the island known to the Americans as the "Tokyo Express." He commanded the Japanese force at the last naval battle of the campaign, the battle of Tassafaronga. This was the single greatest Japanese destroyer victory of the war. Later, on December 12, he was wounded when his flagship was sunk on a resupply run. Following this, he was removed from command. Ironically, his skills seemed to have been appreciated more by the US Navy than the IJN, where his pessimistic comments regarding the course of the campaign resulted in his loss of command. He was later promoted to vice admiral, but never given an important command.

Vice Admiral **Abe Hiroaki** was a 1911 graduate of Eta Jima and spent his career almost entirely in surface units. He achieved flag rank in 1938, and began the war as commander of Sentai 8 (a squadron of Japan's latest heavy cruisers) which were assigned to screen the IJN's main carrier force. Abe fought with the carriers at Midway, during which he assumed temporary command of the battle after the commander of the carrier fleet was forced to depart his flagship. He held important commands during the Guadalcanal campaign, including the Vanguard Force at both the battle of Eastern Solomons in August and again at Santa Cruz in October. Abe was promoted to vice admiral on November 1, 1942, and placed in charge of the Henderson Field bombardment force for the major Japanese November offensive. At the First Naval Battle of Guadalcanal, he was surprised by the Americans. He not only failed to perform his mission, but also lost the first Japanese battleship of the war. As a consequence, he was forced to resign from the IJN in disgrace. On November 14, he was relieved of command and forced to face a Board of Inquiry over the loss of his flagship, the battleship *Hiei*. He was reassigned to the Naval General Staff in December and retired on March 20, 1943.

# US COMMANDERS

The father of the Guadalcanal campaign and the primary figure behind all US naval strategy during World War II was Admiral **Ernest J. King**. After duty on surface ships and submarines, he transferred to naval aviation in 1926. He earned his wings in 1927, and commanded the carrier *Lexington* in 1930. In 1933, he was promoted to flag and assigned to the Bureau of Aeronautics. In 1938, he was promoted to vice admiral and took command of the Pacific Fleet's carriers. In 1939, his career was all but over when instead of being selected for Chief of Naval Operations, he was posted to the General Board. However, as war approached, his undeniable toughness and leadership skills brought him out of irrelevance in January 1941 when he was appointed as the Commander of the Atlantic Fleet. After Pearl Harbor, King was named the Commander-in-Chief US Fleet and in March he was also appointed as Chief of Naval Operations, giving him authority over all American naval strategy and operations.

He did not hesitate to use this authority and constantly worked to expand the US Navy's freedom of action in the Pacific, which under the "Germany First" strategy, was defined as a secondary theater. The Guadalcanal campaign was entirely of King's making. This was a bold, if risky operation which caught the Japanese entirely by surprise. The knowledge that Guadalcanal resulted in an important American victory makes it easy to forget how large a risk King was running when he launched his offensive. Up until the

Admiral Chester Nimitz (left) and Admiral Ernest King on June 30, 1942, as Nimitz received the Distinguished Service Medal for his leadership during the battles of Coral Sea and Midway. Nimitz played a supporting role during the Guadalcanal campaign. King was the originator of the entire concept of an early counteroffensive to roll back Japanese gains in the South Pacific. (Naval History and Heritage Command, NH 58409)

Admiral Chester Nimitz (pictured in 1942) though commander of the Pacific Fleet, did not exert direct control of the Guadalcanal campaign. He was responsible for keeping the battle resourced and he played a key role by relieving his South Pacific commander during a key stage of the battle. (Naval History and Heritage Command, 80-G-466244)

Vice Admiral Robert Ghormley, photographed in 1942. His direction of the Guadalcanal campaign lacked direction and energy and he was replaced in mid-October. (Naval History and Heritage Command, 80-G-12864-A)

naval battles of mid-November, there was the real possibility of an American defeat. Not only would this have had serious implications for the course of the war, but for King personally.

The commander of the US Pacific Fleet after the attack on Pearl Harbor was Admiral **Chester Nimitz.** His early career was spent mainly in submarines, but later he served on cruisers and battleships. Nimitz was recognized as a capable administrator with the ability to pick good leaders and then give them the authority to accomplish their mission. Early in the war, Nimitz displayed his strategic insight and aggressiveness at Coral Sea and Midway. On April 3, Nimitz was appointed as Commander-in-Chief of the Pacific Ocean Areas in addition to his duties as Commander of the Pacific Fleet. This made him responsible for the execution of King's ambitious offensive plans in the South Pacific. However, it is important to note that Nimitz played no role in originating the plan for offensive operations in the South Pacific, and he did not direct operations there since this was the responsibility of the Commander, South Pacific Area. Nimitz played little direct role in battle, other than to ensure a constant flow of reinforcements for the campaign. His most important contribution to the effort was the timely relief of Ghormley in October.

Vice Admiral **Robert Ghormley** assumed the post as Commander, South Pacific Area on June 19. He held this position up until October 18, so he was in overall command during only two of the five major naval surface battles of the campaign. Ghormley has been described as possessing intelligence and a gift for diplomacy, but his direction of the campaign was weak and indecisive. For example, he gave the Japanese undisputed nighttime use of the waters around Guadalcanal from early August until mid-October. Ghormley was a controversial figure and it is easy to blame him for the precarious American position on Guadalcanal. Ghormley had to contend with many severe challenges – a barely workable command structure, limited resources, and, most of all, a tenuous logistical situation. Nevertheless, it is clear that his lack of command experience fed a lack of decisiveness that brought the campaign to the brink of disaster. His continued concern for the protection of his rear areas at the expense of reinforcing Guadalcanal demonstrated he did not fully understand his mission. His saving grace was that the Japanese leadership was even more indecisive.

Vice Admiral **William F. Halsey** relieved Ghormley as Commander, South Pacific Area on October 18, 1942. Halsey began his career primarily in destroyers but in 1934 switched to naval aviation. In June 1940 he was promoted to vice admiral and was the senior ranking carrier commander in the Pacific Fleet. In several early-war carrier raids, he showed his aggressive style, though he missed Coral Sea and Midway. When Nimitz was looking for a leader to breathe energy into the flagging Guadalcanal campaign, the natural choice was Halsey. The selection was inspired and Halsey provided an immediate boost to American morale at a critical juncture in the campaign. He made a promise to support the Marines ashore with everything he had. This resulted in the battle of Santa Cruz in late October when he risked his last two carriers beyond the effective range of land-based air cover. In November, with the campaign in the balance, he did not hesitate to commit his last surface units to protect the airfield. Guadalcanal was Halsey's finest hour. Later in the war, his penchant for sloppy staff work and taking risks would be displayed again.

The commander of the Amphibious Force South Pacific was Rear Admiral **Richmond Kelly Turner**. He was a 1908 graduate of the Naval Academy and spent his early career on destroyers and battleships. Subsequently, he trained as an aviator and remained in various aviation billets until 1935. Following a tour at the Naval War College, he commanded the heavy cruiser *Astoria* from 1938–40. From 1940–42, he served as Director of the War Plans Division and also as assistant chief of staff to King from 1941–42. King made him Commander Amphibious Force South Pacific in time to conduct his offensive in the Solomons. In this capacity, Turner was responsible for the tactical conduct of operations around Guadalcanal, with the exception of the carrier task forces. His misreading of Japanese intentions in the days after the initial landing led directly to the disaster at Savo Island. After Savo, he became a stalwart, making up for Ghormley's lack of aggression. Savo Island aside, Turner proved an aggressive and capable commander and became the premier practitioner of amphibious warfare in the Pacific.

Admiral William Halsey (right) with Nimitz on a repair ship at Espiritu Santo on January 20, 1943. Halsey took over control of the campaign before the Japanese offensive in October, defeating that operation and the final Japanese onslaught in November. His total commitment to supporting the Marines on the island was a key to victory. (Naval History and Heritage Command, 80-G-34822)

Rear Admiral **Norman Scott** was the first US Navy officer to beat the Japanese in a major surface battle during the Pacific War. Graduating from the Naval Academy in 1911, he was the Executive Officer aboard a destroyer that was sunk by German submarine attack in December 1917 and was commended for his performance. Following promotion to captain, he was commanding officer of heavy cruiser *Pensacola* until shortly after Pearl Harbor. Captain Scott was assigned to the staff of Admiral King during the first months of 1942. After promotion to rear admiral in May, he was granted his wish of being posted to a combat command in the Pacific. Scott commanded a surface task group for the first three months of the Guadalcanal campaign, but missed the action at the battles of Savo Island and Eastern Solomons. On the night of October 11–12, Scott got his chance to engage the Japanese. The result was the first Japanese defeat in a night action. Scott's performance at the battle of Cape Esperance was far from perfect, but he had demonstrated that the IJN could be beaten, even at night. His victory was made possible by taking the Japanese by surprise and the implementation of a clear battle plan. In November, command of the American surface task group operating off Guadalcanal was given to Rear Admiral Daniel Callaghan. Undoubtedly, Scott would have been the better choice with his six months' sea experience and his victory at Cape Esperance behind him,

Rear Admiral Richmond Turner on the bridge of attack transport *McCawley* during the initial phases of the Guadalcanal campaign. With him is the commander of the 1st Marine Division, Major General Vandegrift. These two men formed a capable team, which was instrumental in forging victory. (Naval History and Heritage Command, 80-CF-112-4-63)

Norman Scott, shown here as a captain, was the first American admiral to defeat the Japanese in a night battle. Following his victory at Cape Esperance, he was killed in the First Naval Battle of Guadalcanal. (Naval History and Heritage Command, 80-G-20823)

but he was 15 days junior to Callaghan on the seniority list. As deputy commander to Callaghan during the night action known as the First Naval Battle of Guadalcanal on November 13, Scott was killed when his flagship was struck by gunfire. For his actions in the October and November battles, Scott was posthumously awarded the Medal of Honor.

Rear Admiral **Daniel Judson Callaghan** was a 1911 graduate of the Naval Academy. He spent most of his early career on battleship duty. In 1936, he was assigned as executive officer of heavy cruiser *Portland* and then was assigned to the staff of the Pacific Fleet's cruiser force. Following this, he was the Naval Aide to President Roosevelt from 1938–41. In May 1941, he assumed command of heavy cruiser *San Francisco*. In June 1942, Callaghan was assigned as chief of staff to Ghormley. When Halsey took over from Ghormley he brought in his own chief of staff which left Callaghan without a job. Turner decided to use him to command his surface support group, and he relieved Scott when the two forces joined up off of Guadalcanal in November. Callaghan was in command at the First Naval Battle of Guadalcanal and ordered to stop a battleship bombardment of the airfield. Callaghan seemed under no illusion about the fate of his command against a Japanese force with two battleships, but he bravely led his force directly at the oncoming Japanese. However, his bungled handling of the battle undoubtedly increased its cost to the Americans. Callaghan was killed in this action.

Rear Admiral **Willis Augustus Lee** played a critical role in the campaign when he was entrusted by Halsey with the only two operational modern battleships in the Pacific during the Second Naval Battle of Guadalcanal. Lee was a 1908 graduate of the Naval Academy and spent World War I on destroyers. After commanding several destroyers, he moved to cruisers, commanding light cruiser *Concord*, and then held various staff positions, including assistant chief of staff to King. He assumed command of Battleship Division 6 in August 1942, which would eventually lead him to his fateful spot on the bridge of battleship *Washington* in Iron Bottom Sound on the night of November 14–15. He was known as a gunnery expert and was among the first to embrace the use of radar fully. His performance at the Second Naval Battle of Guadalcanal has been acknowledged as superb. It must be also acknowledged that his victory owed a great deal to good luck as well, as none of the many Japanese torpedoes fired at his two battleships hit its target. Lee himself made no bones about his victory being due to the possession of radar, and not to any American edge in skill or training. He went on after Guadalcanal to command fast battleships throughout the war until being assigned in 1945 to investigate methods to combat the kamikaze threat. He died before the end of the war.

Rear Admiral **Carleton Herbert Wright** was a 1912 graduate of the Naval Academy. Following a varied career that focused on mine warfare, he commanded the heavy cruiser *Augusta* in 1941 and then served as commander

Daniel Callaghan pictured as a captain at Ghormley's headquarters in 1942. As a rear admiral, he led the American surface force at the First Naval Battle of Guadalcanal where his lack of control over the battle led to a close-range slugfest with heavy American losses. He did succeed in thwarting the planned Japanese bombardment of Henderson Field. (Naval History and Heritage Command, 80-G-11671)

Rear Admiral Willis Lee pictured on board his flagship *Washington*. His adept handling of *Washington* during the Second Naval Battle of Guadalcanal gained victory for the Americans. (Naval History and Heritage Command, NH 48283)

Carleton Wright, pictured on the left when he was captain of heavy cruiser *Augusta* in September 1941, accompanying Secretary of the Navy Frank Knox on an inspection of his ship. Wright's background in cruisers did nothing to help him in November 1942 when his task force was decimated by Japanese torpedoes. (Naval History and Heritage Command, NH 50323)

of cruiser task forces in the Pacific Fleet from July to November 1942. His first independent command was Task Force 67 at the battle of Tassafaronga in which his cruiser force was sharply defeated by a smaller Japanese destroyer force. Wright took full responsibility for the disaster, as it was his indecision which, more than any other factor, led to defeat. Remarkably, after his humiliation at Tassafaronga, Wright returned to command a cruiser division in the Aleutians and Gilberts campaigns. More amazing was his award of the Navy Cross (the second-highest Navy award for valor) after the battle.

# OPPOSING FLEETS

For decades before the opening of the Pacific war, both navies had planned, equipped and trained for a massive fleet engagement somewhere in the Central Pacific, in which battleships would take center stage. Within this construct, firmly shared by both sides, other fleet elements including aircraft carriers, cruiser and destroyer forces, and submarines were expected to play important roles, but the big guns aboard the battleships were seen as the final arbiters.

The naval campaign of Guadalcanal in no way mirrored the expectation that battleships would play a decisive role. In fact, battleships clashed only once during the entire campaign, and then only in small numbers. The naval battles off Guadalcanal were primarily fought by cruisers and destroyers, with all combat occurring at night. Because of the Japanese emphasis on night combat before the war, they initially held the advantage in the campaign. However, making up for the deficient American night combat doctrine was their technological superiority in the area of radar. Guadalcanal forced both sides to adapt, but the Japanese advantage in night combat was still evident by the end of the campaign.

Adding to the challenge for the Americans was the overall balance of naval power in the Pacific at the start of the campaign. While Midway had reduced the Japanese advantage in carriers, it did little to reduce the IJN's large surface force. At the start of the campaign, the Japanese held a clear advantage in surface force as indicated in this table:

| Pacific naval strength August 1942 | | | | | |
|---|---|---|---|---|---|
| | Carriers (heavy/light) | Battleships (new/old) | Heavy Cruisers | Light Cruisers | Destroyers (new/old) |
| Japanese | 4/3 | 1/10 | 17 | 17 | 67/39 |
| American | 4/0 | 1/7 | 14 | 13 | 59/21 |

The overall size of the US Navy was larger when the Atlantic Fleet was factored in. Select units of the Atlantic fleet were transferred to the Pacific during the battle, and added to this were a growing number of newly built ships from American shipyards, some of which were already reaching the theater before the end of the campaign.

# THE IMPERIAL JAPANESE NAVY

## Capital ships

Despite myth, the Japanese carrier force was not destroyed at Midway. It was in the process of reorganization when the Guadalcanal campaign started and by late August could throw a carrier division with two heavy and one light carrier into battle. The first carrier battle at Eastern Solomons resulted in heavy aircrew losses and the loss of the light carrier. The next major operation by the carrier force was not until late October when Yamamoto gathered four heavy and one light carrier. The resulting battle of Santa Cruz was a Japanese victory, but one heavy and one light carrier suffered battle damage and another heavy carrier was withdrawn back to Japan by Yamamoto. This left just two converted carriers to conduct the rest of the campaign, which proved insufficient to the task. The fragility of the Japanese carrier force placed the burden of the campaign on land-based aircraft operating primarily from Rabaul, and the IJN's surface units.

Going into the Guadalcanal campaign, the Japanese battle line had suffered no damage. With the addition of the superbattleship *Yamato* in February 1942, a total of 11 battleships were available to Yamamoto. Of these, only four, the fast battleships of the Kongo class, were actively employed during the campaign. The high speed of the Kongos made them ideal for operations in the Solomons and since they had been a key component of Japanese nightfighting formations, they were familiar with Japanese nightfighting tactics. Of the six other older battleships, only one even deployed to Truk and it was never active off Guadalcanal. The *Yamato* was used as Yamamoto's flagship at Truk and was never committed to the battles off Guadalcanal. If there was ever a point in the war where Japanese battleships could have been employed to good effect, it was Guadalcanal. The most successful Japanese battleship action of the war was not against American battleships, but against the airfield on Guadalcanal in October. Yamamoto did not consider repeating this bombardment on a larger scale, most likely because of his concern to keep the battle line intact for a possible future clash with their American counterparts.

*Kongo* was the lead ship of a class of four fast battleships. She is shown here in 1936 after her second reconstruction. Originally designed as battle cruisers, the Kongo class was modernized between the wars but still retained a relatively light scale of armored protection. These 32,000-ton ships were heavily used in the Guadalcanal campaign and participated in the October bombardment of Henderson Field that temporarily neutralized the airfield. (Yamato Museum, 071390)

Battleship *Kirishima* pictured in 1939 with carrier *Akagi* behind. The speed of the four Kongo-class units not only made them useful as carrier screening units, but also as the centerpiece of bombardment groups against Henderson Field on Guadalcanal. (Yamato Museum, 071228)

## Cruisers

Since battleships were rarely committed to action off Guadalcanal, heavy cruisers were routinely the largest Japanese units deployed to the island. Of the 18 heavy cruisers with which the Japanese began the war, 16 were still available for operations at the start of the campaign. Japanese heavy cruisers were formidable fighting units, with a heavy-gun armament and a heavy-torpedo battery, and were designed to play a central role in Japanese nightfighting doctrine. The Japanese did not bother to adhere strictly to treaty weight limitations, so their ships were also generally better armored than their American counterparts.

Three heavy cruisers of Sentai 6, as seen from *Kinugasa*. Despite the fact that these were the oldest heavy cruisers in the IJN, dating from 1926, these ships were well-armed and manned by well-trained crews. Sentai 6 provided the muscle in the Japanese victory at Savo Island. (Yamato Museum, O-0003)

21

*Takao*, shown here in 1939, was among the most powerful heavy cruisers in the world at the start of the Guadalcanal campaign. Very heavily armed, she carried ten 8in. guns and 16 24in. torpedo tubes. Her first and only surface action during the campaign was at the Second Naval Battle of Guadalcanal where she pummeled an American battleship with her guns but scored no success with her torpedoes. (Yamato Museum, 070345)

The Japanese actually completed four heavy cruisers before the signature of the Washington Naval Treaty. These included two ships of the Furutaka class and two Aoba-class units. The Furutaka class set the tone for future Japanese cruisers. The design featured heavy gun and torpedo batteries and high speed. Protection was clearly secondary to firepower.

The next class of Japanese heavy cruisers, the four-ship Myoko class, was the best of the early Washington Treaty designs. In part because the design exceeded the 10,000-ton limit, the Japanese were able to give the ships ten 8in. guns and eventually 16 torpedo tubes. The next class represented the epitome of Treaty Cruiser designs. The four ships of the Takao class possessed the same heavy armament as the Myokos and also possessed increased armor protection. All four of these ships were active off Guadalcanal.

The final two classes of Japanese heavy cruisers actually began as light cruisers. With the expiration of the London Naval Treaty, the four units of the Mogami class were rearmed with 8in. guns in 1939. The ships were as heavily armored as a heavy cruiser. The final class of Japanese heavy cruisers was laid down in 1934 and completed in 1938–39. This was the two-ship Tone class, which had extensive aircraft handling capabilities. Despite the fact that these were the most heavily armored Japanese heavy cruisers and still carried a substantial torpedo armament, these ships were retained as carrier screening ships and never saw action off Guadalcanal.

Japanese heavy cruisers were the most potent nightfighting units in the world at the start of the Guadalcanal campaign. These ships were extremely well armed, with between six and ten 8in. guns and between eight and 16 torpedo tubes with as many reloads. The Japanese decision to retain torpedoes on their heavy cruisers, unlike the Americans, paid off at Guadalcanal.

### Destroyers

Like their heavy cruisers, Japanese destroyers were designed primarily with night combat in mind. Destroyers played a prominent role in the attrition tactics that the Japanese planned in advance of the main fleet action between battle lines. Since they possessed minimal antiair and antisubmarine capabilities, Japanese destroyers were not as well balanced as their American counterparts, but they were superb torpedo boats, well suited for night combat.

To carry out their nightfighting duties, Japanese destroyers possessed high speed and heavy armament. The Fubuki class or "Special Type" were

Destroyer *Fubuki* was the lead ship in a class of "Special Type" destroyers that were the most powerful destroyers in the world when they entered service. Completed in 1928, *Fubuki* carried six 5in. guns in three twin-gun unarmored mounts and nine torpedo tubes in three mounts. *Fubuki* was sunk by gunfire at the battle of Cape Esperance. (Yamato Museum, 071898)

the most powerful destroyers in the world when introduced in 1927. This class carried a heavy gun armament of six 5in. guns in three enclosed mounts and an impressive torpedo armament of nine torpedo tubes with reloads. This basic design was retained for the next five classes of Japanese destroyers. All of these had at least five 5in. guns and six to eight torpedo tubes with a comparable number of reloads.

## Torpedoes

The success of Japanese torpedo tactics was due in large measure to the extraordinary torpedo that they used. The Japanese desired a long-range torpedo to make their nightfighting tactics more effective. Accordingly, they put much effort into perfecting an oxygen-propelled torpedo which had the potential to increase range greatly, with the added attractions of allowing for a larger warhead and offering nearly wakeless running. Despite the risks of using oxygen as a propellant in a shipboard environment, the Japanese persevered and by 1932 had a workable weapon. Known as the Type 93 (the designation comes from the year of its official adoption – 1933 – which was the year 2593 on the Japanese calendar), it was eventually fitted on all modern destroyers, heavy cruisers, and select light cruisers. It was considered a top-secret weapon by the Japanese, and its existence was unknown to the Americans at the start of the Guadalcanal campaign. The table below shows the clear superiority of the Type 93 over its American counterpart.

| American and Japanese destroyer-launched torpedoes | Mark 15 (USN) | Type 93 (IJN) |
|---|---|---|
| Length | 22ft 7in. | 29ft 6in. |
| Diameter | 21in. | 24in. |
| Weight | 3,438lb | 5,940lb |
| Warhead | 494lb | 1,078lb |
| Propulsion | Steam | Oxygen |
| Speed | 28/34/46kts | 36/40/48kts |
| Range | 15,000/10,000/6,000yd | 43,700/35,000/21,900yd |

The Type 93 oxygen-propelled torpedo was the most capable weapon of its type during the Guadalcanal campaign. It was the basis for Japanese night combat tactics and proved an effective ship-killer throughout the campaign. Despite its many successes, American naval commanders remained ignorant of its true capabilities. (Naval History and Heritage Command, NH 94125)

### Imperial Japanese Navy nightfighting doctrine

Unlike the US Navy, IJN nightfighting tactics revolved around the use of the torpedo. With the introduction of the Type 93 torpedo, the Japanese reworked their nightfighting tactics to take advantage of the long range of the new weapon. The new system called for "long-distance concealed firing" by heavy cruisers, after which the destroyer squadrons would close and complete the destruction of the enemy. Destroyers were trained to fire their first torpedo load, then disengage, reload within 15 minutes, and fire a second barrage.

The Japanese also put great thought and effort into developing all the tools required to conduct night fighting. One area of particular importance was in optics. In the period preceding the Pacific War, the Japanese developed and produced world-class optical devices. Among these were powerful binoculars with sophisticated magnification and light-gathering capabilities. The higher the quality and the bigger the lens, the more capable these optics were at night. The superiority of Japanese optics partially counterbalanced the Japanese lack of radar. The Japanese also developed star shells and flares, including a parachute-suspended type in 1935, and Japanese guns used smokeless powder to avoid disclosing the location of the firing ship.

All considered, the IJN entered the campaign as the most capable nightfighting force in the world. This was the result of superior doctrine, better nightfighting weapons and equipment and the fact that Japanese cruiser and destroyer crews were better trained than their American counterparts.

Heavy cruiser *Chokai* firing an 8in. broadside in 1933. The IJN's cruiser crews were extremely skilled in the use of gunnery as was evident at Savo Island, where gunfire was the principal form of destruction against the four Allied heavy cruisers that were sunk. (Naval History and Heritage Command, NH 73024)

# THE UNITED STATES NAVY

## Capital ships

At the start of the campaign, the US Navy possessed five fleet carriers. One of these was in the Atlantic and was deemed unsuitable for combat operations in the Pacific. Since no more carriers would be available for the remainder of 1942, these few ships had to be used judiciously. This meant they were employed only during major operations, or in response to major Japanese offensives. The Americans had the supreme advantage of an airfield on Guadalcanal, which meant the carriers could be kept in readiness and committed only when absolutely necessary. A portion of the surface fleet had to be devoted to screening duties for the carriers, including the most modern battleships, which were very useful as antiaircraft platforms. The fact that so few carriers were available put the onus of operations at Guadalcanal on the surface combatants.

Despite myth, the American battle line was not destroyed at Pearl Harbor. Though five battleships were sunk in the attack, by the early months of 1942, seven old battleships were available for operations. These were reinforced by the two modern units of the North Carolina class and the first units of the South Dakota class. King kept pressing Nimitz to employ the older battleships

Light cruiser *Sendai* in 1939 with a Hatsuharu-class destroyer. Unlike American light cruisers, Japanese light cruisers were designed as flagships for destroyer squadrons and were relatively lightly armed, usually with seven single 5.5in. guns and eight torpedo tubes. *Sendai* was active off Guadalcanal and was a participant in the Second Naval Battle of Guadalcanal where she was targeted by 16in. radar-directed battleship fire but was undamaged. (Yamato Museum, 062578)

*Enterprise*, shown here in November after the Naval Battles for Guadalcanal, played a central role in the campaign. She was damaged at both the battle of Eastern Solomons and Santa Cruz, but she survived until the climactic battles in November when her aircraft played a key role in destroying the large Japanese convoy heading to the island. (Naval History and Heritage Command, 19-N-47849)

North Carolina was the lead ship of a class of two battleships, which in 1942 were arguably the most powerful in the world. After being assigned carrier screening duties early in the campaign, North Carolina was torpedoed by a Japanese submarine on September 15 and missed the decisive phase of the campaign. (Naval History and Heritage Command, NH 80988)

in the campaign, but Nimitz declined because of concerns about their underwater protection, and the large fuel requirements needed to send them to the South Pacific. However, the modern North Carolina units (*North Carolina* and *Washington*) were employed in the campaign, serving primarily as screening units in the carrier task forces. American admirals did not think it advisable to use them in the constrained waters around Guadalcanal, especially at night, owing to the extreme torpedo threat. These ships were designed for long-range gunnery duels with their 16in. rifles in daytime, not for night combat. However, when pressed into service around the island in November, their radar-controlled gunnery proved devastating.

### Cruisers

The US Navy's prewar-built cruisers carried the primary burden of combat during the Guadalcanal campaign. The number and characteristics of American cruisers were shaped by the series of naval treaties in effect during the period between the wars. The Washington Naval Treaty, signed in 1922, did not limit the numbers of cruisers that could be built, but did limit their maximum size (10,000 tons) and maximum gun size (8in.) that could be carried. The London Naval Treaty of 1930 dictated the total cruiser tonnage allocated to the major naval powers. The effect of these treaties was to limit the US Navy to 18 heavy cruisers and nine large light cruisers with 6in. guns. Most of these saw action off Guadalcanal.

Heavy cruiser *Salt Lake City* pictured in the early 1930s. The lightly armored ship was damaged by three hits at the battle of Cape Esperance and was under repair until the following March when she returned to service at the battle of the Komandorski Islands. (Naval History and Heritage Command, NH-85083)

The 10,000-ton limit forced American naval designers to make choices between protection, firepower, and speed in the so-called "Treaty Cruisers." The design of the early American Treaty Cruisers clearly showed a preference for firepower over protection. The two ships of the Pensacola class, *Pensacola* and *Salt Lake City*, each carried ten 8in. and eight 5in. dual-purpose guns. The ships were actually 900 tons underweight and overall armored protection was deficient. Also, before the war, these ships, and every other American heavy cruiser, had their torpedo tubes removed.

Construction work on the next class attempted to remedy some of the weaknesses of the Pensacola class. The five ships of the Northampton class (*Northampton, Chester, Louisville, Chicago, Houston* and *Augusta*) were more heavily armored, and still carried nine 8in. guns in three triple turrets. The next two classes of cruisers were more balanced designs. The two-ship Portland class (*Portland* and *Indianapolis*) was better armored and carried the same main battery as the Portland class. The best American prewar heavy cruiser design was the six-ship New Orleans class. These ships had a good mix of protection, firepower and speed, with the emphasis placed on protection. Five of these ships saw service in the campaign (*Astoria, Minneapolis, New Orleans, Quincy* and *Vincennes*), with three being lost. Each ship carried nine 8in. guns in three triple turrets and eight single dual-purpose 5in. guns. By the time of the Guadalcanal campaign, all heavy cruisers carried radar.

Construction of prewar heavy cruisers ceased after the completion of the last New Orleans-class ship and the unique *Wichita*. Having filled their allotted heavy cruiser tonnage, the Americans turned to construction of light cruisers which were restricted to having guns no larger than 6in. The new 6in. gun cruisers, known as the Brooklyn class, were as heavily armored as the latest heavy cruisers and carried a large battery of 15 6in. guns. This new gun used semi-fixed ammunition that permitted a very high rate of fire. All these ships carried radar. Of the nine Brooklyn- and near-sister St Louis-class units, three, *Boise, Honolulu* and *Helena* saw service in the South Pacific during the Guadalcanal campaign.

Beginning in December 1941, another class of light cruisers, named after the lead ship *Atlanta*, entered service. These ships were originally designed as scout cruisers and were heavily armed with eight twin 5in. mounts and torpedoes. This armament made them ideally suited as antiaircraft platforms,

but their light armor made them ill-suited for surface combat. Four ships of the class were active during the Guadalcanal campaign; two of these were engaged in surface combat and both were sunk.

### Destroyers

The interwar naval treaties also impacted on American destroyer designs and numbers. The London Naval Treaty of 1930 placed limits on overall destroyer construction and restricted the maximum size of destroyers. Just as for cruiser construction, designers faced difficult choices with regard to placing heavier armament, greater endurance, and superior sea-keeping qualities on larger destroyers, or producing a greater number of smaller destroyers where compromises had to be made. Generally, American designers favored larger designs with a heavy gun armament.

The US Navy saw destroyers as more than just torpedo boats. They also needed a heavy gun armament to defeat Japanese destroyer attacks against the battle line and to contribute to fleet air defense against Japanese aircraft. Torpedo armament was also an important design consideration, since this was the only way a destroyer could inflict serious damage on enemy heavy units. A typical prewar American destroyer was the 18-unit Mahan class, all of which saw action in the Pacific. These ships had a standard displacement of 1,500 tons and carried five 5in. guns and 12 torpedo tubes. Late in the campaign, the first American destroyer class designed totally free of treaty restrictions reached the Solomons. This was the Fletcher class, which presented a good mix of speed (38 knots), and offensive and defensive capabilities. Each ship carried five 5in. guns, and ten torpedo tubes. Like all other American destroyers, the Fletchers carried radar.

The primary weapon of the destroyer in surface combat was its torpedo. American destroyers were severely handicapped by the performance of their inferior torpedoes, and during the Guadalcanal campaign these problems were not even recognized, much less addressed. The standard American destroyer torpedo was the Mark 15. When compared with the standard Japanese torpedo, it was markedly inferior. Added to this, the Mark 15 was unreliable, since it suffered from faulty magnetic fuses and a tendency to run well below its set depth. The result was that the main weapon of American destroyers was defective throughout the campaign. In turn, this reinforced the prevailing view that the gun, not the torpedo, was the US Navy's primary weapon of decision.

## Radar

The biggest advantage possessed by the Americans in the night surface battles fought during the campaign was radar. It had significant impact on a number of battles. However, at the start of the campaign American radars were fairly primitive and commanders did not fully understand their use. The first radar in widespread use was the SC-2. This was fitted aboard both destroyers and cruisers and had an approximate range, under ideal conditions, of six miles against a destroyer-sized target. The next set introduced was the SG radar, which was designed as a surface search radar. It was the first surface search set to incorporate a plan position indicator (PPI) display. The PPI provided a radar "map" of the area, making it much easier to use and interpret. Under ideal conditions, the SG radar could detect a destroyer-sized target at 15 miles.

In addition to providing detection of an approaching enemy at extended ranges, the US Navy was also developing tactics to use radar to direct gunnery. This had great potential to increase the effectiveness of night gunnery since visibility was no longer a factor. However, radar was not infallible. It was often unable to break out different targets located close together, maneuvering rapidly, or located close to land. Even more significant was the inability of radar to tell the difference between enemy ships and shell splashes around them after they had been taken under fire. This led to the phenomenon known as "chasing splashes" since shell splashes in front of the target were often the strongest returns, which prompted the radar operator to target them. This allowed the real target to move away, only to be picked up again as a new target after the operator stopped targeting his own splashes.

The Fletcher class was the largest class of fleet destroyers ever built. With their combination of firepower, speed and advanced electronics, these ships became deadly threats to the IJN. (Naval History and Heritage Command, NH-53916)

Light cruiser *Juneau* in June 1942. The Atlanta-class unit had a short career from February until November 1942. She was sunk by a submarine torpedo immediately following the Second Naval Battle of Guadalcanal and all but ten of her crew of 693 died. (Naval History and Heritage Command, 19-N-31263)

By November 1942, the first ships of the new Fletcher class began to reach the South Pacific. This is the lead ship *Fletcher*, pictured in July 1942. This view shows the ship's five 5in. guns and two quintuple torpedo launchers. Perhaps more importantly, the ship had a full radar suit including the modern SG surface search radar (the small curved device on the mainmast). (Naval History and Heritage Command, 19-N-31243)

## *US Navy nightfighting doctrine*

Going into the Guadalcanal campaign, American nightfighting doctrine was inadequate. This was in spite of the fact that it was recognized that part of any decisive surface engagement would be fought at night and that night tactics had been under development since 1932. American night tactics stressed gun combat and featured a flawed torpedo doctrine. This meant that commanders during the Guadalcanal campaign devised tactics geared to cruiser gunnery while ignoring the offensive potential of destroyers.

This imbalance stemmed from an emphasis on so-called "Major Tactics" which were devised and practiced as part of the expected decisive engagement between opposing battle lines. "Minor Tactics" for light units were not seen as important. Cruisers and destroyers were well drilled in forcing a hole in the enemy screen to allow destroyers to attack enemy battleships at close range with torpedoes. Destroyer gunfire was to be directed at the enemy battleship's bridge and superstructure to reduce its defensive fire. This tactic reinforced the notion that only battleships were worthy of torpedo attack and that the targets would be slow and well illuminated. This had little resemblance to actual conditions off Guadalcanal.

Though American torpedo tactics and torpedoes were deficient, American gunnery was more effective. Early in the Guadalcanal campaign, the firepower of the heavy cruiser with its heavier 8in. shell was preferred since it had the penetrative power to defeat Japanese heavy cruisers. The fast-firing 6in. guns on the light cruisers were preferred against destroyers because of their volume of fire. Using radar, American admirals were convinced that they could engage a target at 10,000 yards and destroy it before it could fire torpedoes. Unfortunately for the Americans, this was less than the effective range of the Japanese Type 93 torpedo. The Americans remained ignorant of the true capabilities of the Type 93 throughout the campaign.

# OPPOSING PLANS

## JAPANESE PLANS

Following Midway, the Japanese did not expect any American offensive moves in the Pacific. However, King's limited counteroffensive caught the Japanese totally by surprise. As will be recounted shortly, the American landing on August 7 did prompt a sharp response by the local Japanese commander, but to throw the Americans off the island would require a unified plan by both the Imperial Army and Navy. Since this was the first Allied attempt to regain lost territory, it was a test of Japan's basic war strategy of repelling any Allied assault on the Japanese perimeter, and making the cost of any failed Allied offensive so prohibitive that the Americans would eventually seek a negotiated peace, leaving Japan with her conquests.

The first meeting of the Army and Navy Sections of the Imperial General Headquarters took place on August 7. Even at this earliest meeting the

Henderson Field in August 1942. Note the aircraft on the left and the many bomb and shell craters all around. Possession of the airfield was the key to victory in the Guadalcanal campaign. (Naval History and Heritage Command, 80-G-16312)

pattern of underestimating the strength of the American offensive was apparent. The first assessment by the Japanese was that the attack was only a reconnaissance in force. Upon receiving reports from the Japanese air attacks on August 7 of 30 transports present off Guadalcanal, wiser heads prevailed and the American move was assessed to be a divisional-sized attack. On August 10, the heads of the Naval and Army General Staffs agreed to a plan to deal with the incursion. Ongoing operations to occupy Port Moresby on New Guinea would still be given priority, but 17th Army under General Hyakutake Harukichi was assigned the mission to retake Guadalcanal and Tulagi. For this, he was assigned an infantry brigade and two regiments. Of these, only one regiment, located at Guam, was immediately available.

Within days of this plan, the estimate of the American garrison on Guadalcanal had been drastically revised down. This confirmed a pattern of Japanese bending intelligence to preconceived notions of American intentions and capabilities and set up a cycle of piecemeal commitment. The immediate result of this combination of overconfidence and the desire to dislodge the Marines as quickly as possible resulted in the decision to attack with a single battalion (the Ichiki detachment of 917 men) as soon as possible. Since the actual size of the Marine garrison was some 10,000 men, this attack resulted in failure.

On August 20, the first American aircraft arrived on Guadalcanal. Since victory would ultimately be decided by which side could reinforce the island the fastest, the presence of the American airfield made the Japanese task much more difficult. The Americans now dominated the waters around the island during the day, which made the use of transports to bring troops to the island impossible. This was confirmed during the battle of the Eastern Solomons when a small Japanese convoy was turned back by airpower. Over time, it proved impossible for the Japanese to suppress the airfield using bombers from Rabaul or aircraft from carriers.

In mid-September, a Japanese attempt to take the airfield with a brigade failed. This failure seemed to galvanize the Japanese into making a real effort to bring decisive forces to bear. The Naval General Staff saw this as the setting for a decisive battle with the Americans, though this sense of urgency never seems to have filled Yamamoto with the determination to commit all his forces. The recapture of Guadalcanal was now given priority over the New Guinea operation and two divisions were allocated to 17th Army. With these reinforcements, a new attack was planned for about October 20.

These reinforcements were moved to Guadalcanal by a combination of small barges, nightly destroyer runs, and a convoy of transports, which arrived on the island after the airfield was temporarily neutralized by a Japanese battleship bombardment. Yamamoto now made supporting the recapture of the island the primary mission of the Combined Fleet, rather than the destruction of the American fleet. However, when the Japanese ground attack was launched, it again failed.

This set up the decisive phase of the campaign, when the Japanese planned to send a large convoy to the island. To cover this convoy, Yamamoto stepped up air attacks against the airfield and planned to conduct another battleship bombardment to knock out the airfield. The failure of this effort in November was the turning point in the campaign.

# UNITED STATES PLANS

Compared with the Japanese plans, the Americans had a simple set of tasks – occupy the island, keep the airfield open, and react to major Japanese reinforcement operations. As long as the airfield was able to operate aircraft, the Americans dominated the waters around Guadalcanal during the day. This made movement of reinforcements to the island by transports all but impossible.

Since the Japanese were unable to operate near Guadalcanal during the day, they were forced to rely on destroyers to run troops and supplies into the island at night. This was an inefficient means of transport and did not allow the movement of heavy supporting equipment. The Americans were slow to respond to the constant Japanese movement of troops and supplies at night. After the battle of Savo Island, the Japanese were in undisputed control of the waters around Guadalcanal after dark. It was not until mid-October that Ghormley took measures to stop the Tokyo Express, which resulted in the battle of Cape Esperance.

When the Japanese used battleships to neutralize the airfield temporarily in October, the Americans had to take measures to prevent another such bombardment. This was the reason behind the decisive naval battles in November when the Americans threw task forces against Japanese battleship bombardment forces on two occasions.

An American destroyer sails up what would soon be known as Iron Bottom Sound on August 7, 1942. Savo Island is straight ahead in the distance and Cape Esperance on Guadalcanal is on the left. (Naval History and Heritage Command, 80-G-13539)

# THE NAVAL CAMPAIGN FOR GUADALCANAL

## THE BATTLE OF SAVO ISLAND

An American light tank being unloaded from an attack transport ship on August 7, 1942. The landing on Guadalcanal was unopposed and the island's airfield was quickly captured. (Naval History and Heritage Command, 80-G-10973)

The longest naval campaign of the Pacific War began on August 7, 1942 when the United States launched its first offensive of the World War II. The target of the American move was the uncompleted Japanese airfield on the island of Guadalcanal on the southern Solomon Islands. The Marines landed five battalions on Guadalcanal and, against weak resistance, succeeded in capturing the airfield on the afternoon of August 8.

The surprised Japanese garrison on the island was composed of construction troops and was unable to impede the American advance to the airfield. However, Japanese forces in the Rabaul area were quick to respond. The first reaction took the form of an air raid with 27 G4M1 bombers escorted by 18 A6M2 Model 21 fighters. A group of nine D3A dive-bombers was also dispatched to make the 565-mile trip to Guadalcanal, even though these lacked the range to return to Rabaul. One of the fighters turned back, leaving 53 aircraft to attack the naval units off the American beachhead. The attack was an expensive failure with five bombers, two Zeros and all nine dive-bombers being lost in exchange for a single bomb hit on an American destroyer. The defending American fighters suffered heavily, losing nine aircraft, but the Japanese goal of disrupting the landing was unachieved.

The next day, August 8, the Japanese air assault continued. This time, 27 bombers loaded with torpedoes escorted by 15 fighters headed south to Guadalcanal. Unable to find their

primary target, the American carrier force, they turned to hit the beachhead. Twenty-three bombers actually conducted the attack. Against defending American fighters and heavy antiaircraft fire, 18 of the bombers were destroyed, along with two fighters. In exchange, one destroyer was hit by a torpedo (the vessel eventually sank on its return trip to the United States for repairs), and one bomber crashed into a transport, which caused a serious fire, forcing the ship to be scuttled.

The ineffective air attacks were not the only reactions planned by the Japanese. As soon as Mikawa learned of the American landing on Guadalcanal, he resolved to mount a night attack with whatever surface units were available. By 0830hrs on August 7, he ordered his five available heavy cruisers to join at Simpson Harbor at Rabaul. These included his flagship, *Chokai*, and the four ships of Sentai 6 which were anchored at Kavieng out of the range of Allied air attack. Rounding out Mikawa's force were the two old light cruisers of Sentai 18 and a single available, and again old, destroyer. Aside from the four ships of Sentai 6, none of these ships had ever worked together. By 1430hrs, the scratch force had received its orders and, under Mikawa's personal command, sailed out of Simpson Harbor.

As Mikawa headed south, he had little idea of the strength of the American forces around Guadalcanal, and, more importantly, the location of the American carrier force. Long-range aircraft from Rabaul were unable to find the American carriers, but Mikawa did eventually receive information about the location and numbers of Allied ships in the waters off Guadalcanal. A report from one of his cruiser floatplanes indicated that the American force was larger then his own, but Mikawa was sure that the Japanese edge in night tactics would even the odds. At 1300hrs he headed south from his position east of Bougainville Island into the body of water inside the Solomon

On August 8, the Japanese sent 27 G4M1 bombers with torpedoes to attack the invasion shipping of Guadalcanal. Twenty-three of the bombers attacked, and suffered heavy losses. This shows part of that event with the transport *President Jackson* in the foreground with a cruiser and low-hanging antiaircraft bursts in the background. The attack damaged a destroyer and a transport, neither of which survived. (Naval History and Heritage Command, 80-G-K-385)

Islands that would soon be known as "the Slot." His intention was to strike at the American landing force during the night of August 8–9. The Japanese force would pass to the south of Savo Island and enter the waters off Guadalcanal which would soon be known as Iron Bottom Sound after the number of ships which would come to rest there. Upon entering Iron Bottom Sound, the Japanese force would first engage the enemy units located off Guadalcanal before swinging to the north to engage the enemy force off Tulagi. Of note: Mikawa's pre-battle instructions made no mention of attacking the transport fleet.

The Japanese plan counted on gaining surprise. If Mikawa's force was detected early, it could be attacked by American aircraft from the three carriers operating south of Guadalcanal or, even if his force was not attacked by air, it faced a superior Allied surface force once it reached Guadalcanal. The impending disaster for the Allies was directly linked to their inability to provide warning of Mikawa's approach. There were certainly many opportunities to ensure that the Allied ships were ready and waiting for Mikawa off Guadalcanal. The Japanese force was spotted south of the St George Channel by submarine *S-38* about 2000hrs on August 7. The next morning, at 1026hrs, a Royal Australian Air Force (RAAF) Hudson aircraft spotted Mikawa east of Bougainville. The RAAF crew reported the Japanese force as "three cruisers, three destroyers, two seaplane tenders or gunboats" on a southeasterly course at 15 knots. A second Hudson spotted Mikawa again at 1101hrs and gave a report that included two heavy cruisers, two light cruisers and one unknown ship.

The Allied naval force operating off Guadalcanal was under the overall command of Rear Admiral Richmond Turner. Turner appointed British Rear Admiral Victor Crutchley as his deputy. Turner had good reason to believe

On August 8, the Japanese dispatched G4M bombers with torpedoes to attack invasion shipping off Guadalcanal. This view shows the aircraft approaching their targets at low level. The attack was repelled with heavy losses. (Naval History and Heritage Command, 80-G-17066)

that his ships off Guadalcanal would receive adequate warning of a Japanese counterattack. In addition to American and Australian aircraft flying from New Guinea covering the waters south and east of Rabaul, American PBY flying boats and B-17s flew search patterns covering the entire Solomons and the waters to the north of the Solomons against any movement down from the Japanese central Pacific base at Truk. Even after *S-38*'s report of a Japanese force moving south at high speed on August 7, Turner expected that if the Japanese continued south they would be detected by air searches. However, the hastily created American search plan contained several holes, which were exacerbated by problems with weather. The sectors most likely to contact the Japanese were missed owing to weather conditions, and a request for an afternoon search in the most dangerous area was ignored. Mikawa timed his approach carefully in order not to enter the danger area for detection until the late afternoon, well after the morning flights had reached the farthest limits of their patterns. The fact that the searches in the sector most likely to contain the Japanese had not been conducted only reached Turner at 2333hrs on August 8.

The two Hudsons which contacted the Japanese force during the morning were under orders to maintain contact until another aircraft arrived on station. Neither did so. On top of that, their ship identification skills were very poor. The worst part was that the contact reports did not reach Turner until well after the fact; 1900hrs for the first contact and 2130hrs for the second.

Given the lack of contact data after 1101hrs and the misidentification of a Japanese force, which included two seaplane tenders that posed no threat to his beachhead, Turner did nothing to raise the alert status of his ships off Guadalcanal. While his deduction that the Japanese force was intent on setting up a seaplane base on Santa Isabel Island northwest of Guadalcanal was reasonable, given the information at hand, he was guilty of attempting to discern Japanese intentions, while not taking into account their capabilities and preparing for the most dangerous course of action that they might take. His failure to alert his command to the possibility of a Japanese night attack would have tragic consequences.

As flagship of 8th Fleet, heavy cruiser *Chokai* saw continual action during the campaign. This is *Chokai* at Truk in November 1942 with either superbattleship *Yamato* or *Musashi* in the background. *Chokai* was present at Savo Island, and returned to the waters off Guadalcanal to bombard Henderson Field on October 14. She later provided cover for another cruiser force, which bombarded the airfield on November 14; after the bombardment, *Chokai* was lightly damaged by aircraft from *Enterprise*. (Yamato Museum, 070300)

# SAVO ISLAND ORDER OF BATTLE

## IMPERIAL JAPANESE NAVY

| | |
|---|---|
| 8th Fleet Striking Force | Vice Admiral Mikawa Gunichi |
| Flagship | Heavy cruiser *Chokai* |
| Sentai 6 | Rear Admiral Goto Aritomo |
| Heavy cruisers *Aoba, Kinugasa, Kako, Furutaka* | |
| Sentai 18 | |
| Light cruisers *Tenryu, Yubari* | |
| Destroyer *Yunagi* | |

## UNITED STATES NAVY

| | |
|---|---|
| Task Force 62 | Rear Admiral Richmond K. Turner |
| Southern Group | Rear Admiral Victor Crutchley, RN |
| Heavy cruisers *Australia* (RAN), *Canberra* (RAN), *Chicago* | |
| Destroyers *Bagley, Patterson* | |
| Northern Group Captain | Frederick Riefkohl |
| Heavy cruisers *Astoria, Quincy, Vincennes* | |
| Destroyers *Helm, Wilson* | |
| Eastern Group | Rear Admiral Norman Scott |
| Light cruisers *San Juan*, *Hobart* (RAN) | |
| Destroyers *Monssen, Buchanan* | |
| Picket Ships | |
| Destroyers *Blue, Ralph Talbot* | |

The total Allied force of six heavy cruisers, two light cruisers, and eight destroyers possessed the means to deal with Mikawa's smaller force. However, the deployment of the Allied force was too dispersed and therefore subject to defeat in detail. The two destroyers on picket duty north and south of Savo Island were both equipped with radar, but since they could be apart by as much as 20 miles at certain times, there remained a huge gap for the Japanese to enter Iron Bottom Sound undetected. In addition, the picket destroyers were not deployed far enough ahead of the cruiser groups to give adequate warning. On top of this, on the night of the August 8, Crutchley took *Australia* out of position for a conference with Turner. He left the captain of *Chicago* in charge of the Southern Group. When the conference was over, he did not return to the Southern Group, but neglected to tell the commanders of the other groups any of this.

## Savo Island: phase one

Mikawa's luck held as he approached Savo Island. At 2312hrs, he launched four floatplanes to provide information about the Allied deployment and to provide target illumination at the appropriate time. Even the presence of these aircraft above the Allied ships, which were correctly identified as cruiser floatplanes, failed to alert the Allied commanders. At 2400hrs, Mikawa brought his ships to battle stations and increased speed to 26 knots. The first Allied ship encountered was the picket destroyer *Blue* steaming southwest of Savo Island. Lookouts on the lead Japanese ship, *Chokai*, spotted the American ship at over five miles at 0050hrs. Not for the first time Japanese optics would prove superior to American electronics. Mikawa deftly slowed his speed to reduce his wake and *Blue* steamed away to the south.

# The battle of Savo Island

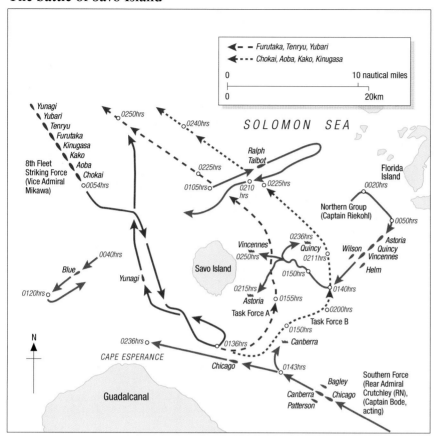

Scale: Furutaka, Tenryu, Yubari; Chokai, Aoba, Kako, Kinugasa

0 ——— 10 nautical miles
0 ——— 20km

SOLOMON SEA

Yunagi
Yubari
Tenryu
Furutaka
Kinugasa
8th Fleet        Kako
Striking Force   Aoba
(Vice Admiral    Chokai
Mikawa)          0054hrs

0250hrs
0240hrs
0225hrs
0105hrs
0210 hrs
0225hrs

Ralph Talbot

Florida Island
0020hrs

Northern Group (Captain Riekohl)
0050hrs

Astoria
0236hrs    Quincy    Wilson    Quincy
Vincennes  0211hrs              Vincennes
0250hrs              Helm

Savo Island

0040hrs
Blue
Yunagi
0120hrs

0150hrs
0215hrs
Astoria    0155hrs
Task Force A

0140hrs
0200hrs
Task Force B
0150hrs
Canberra

N

0236hrs    0136hrs

CAPE ESPERANCE
0143hrs
Chicago
Bagley
Canberra   Chicago
Patterson

Southern Force (Rear Admiral Crutchley (RN), (Captain Bode, acting)

Guadalcanal

Chokai's lookouts remained vigilant when at 0134hrs they spotted destroyer *Jarvis* to port as she exited the area after having been damaged by the earlier air attacks. Just two minutes later, the same lookouts spotted three "cruisers" at over six miles. These were the unsuspecting ships of the Southern Group. The battle opened at 0138hrs with *Chokai* firing four torpedoes at *Canberra*; all missed. *Chokai* opened fire on *Canberra* at 0143hrs. Within minutes, *Furutaka*, *Aoba* and *Kako* joined in; by this time the Southern Group was illuminated by flares dropped by Japanese floatplanes.

Heavy cruiser *Kako* under way in 1940. After an outstanding performance at the battle of Savo Island, *Kako* was sunk the day after the battle by a submarine, with the loss of 43 men. (Naval History and Heritage Command, NH 73014)

Destroyer *Patterson* in May 1942 at Pearl Harbor. *Patterson* was a 1,500-ton Bagley-class destroyer and was present at Savo Island where she was one of the few American ships to put in a creditable performance. After attempting to warn the rest of the American task force, she fought a gun duel with *Tenryu* and *Yunagi*. During this engagement, *Patterson* took a Japanese shell, which knocked out her two aft guns and killed ten men. (Naval History and Heritage Command, 80-G-64754)

*Canberra* was smothered by as many as 24 hits in the first few minutes of the battle. Her captain was mortally wounded, power was quickly lost, and a hit below the waterline created a severe starboard list. Fortunately for the Allies, all of the 11 torpedoes fired at the Australian cruiser missed. The other heavy cruiser in the Southern Group, *Chicago*, mounted an ineffectual response. Her crew was unable to grasp that *Canberra*'s sudden maneuvering meant she was already under attack. At 0147hrs, a torpedo from *Kako* hit the cruiser on her starboard bow. A second torpedo hit the cruiser aft in the machinery spaces, but did not explode. *Chicago* was unable to find any targets for her main battery, but did engage *Tenryu* with her 5in. guns, probably scoring a hit which caused severe personnel casualties. *Chicago* continued to steam to the west and soon exited the engagement. Inexplicably, her captain sent no report of this action. He also neglected to give orders to his two destroyers. *Patterson* engaged at least three Japanese cruisers with gunfire, but was damaged by gunfire in return and was ordered to break off the engagement at 0210hrs. Of all the Allied ships present, destroyer *Patterson* was the most alert and best fought. Destroyer *Bagley* launched an ineffectual torpedo attack and then moved off to the west. In only seven minutes, Mikawa's cruisers had neutralized the Southern Group. None of the ships of the Southern Group bothered to report any of this.

### Savo Island: phase two

The Northern Group, under the command of the skipper of cruiser *Vincennes*, remained oblivious to the presence of Mikawa's force. During the engagement with the Southern Group, the Japanese force had split into two separate columns. To the east was *Chokai*, leading *Aoba*, *Kako*, and *Kinugasa*; the western column included *Yubari*, leading *Tenryu* and *Furutaka*. The only Japanese destroyer, *Yunagi*, was busily engaged in a sporadic gunnery duel with *Jarvis* south of Savo Island.

Previously, *Chokai*'s superb lookouts had spotted at 0138hrs one of the cruisers of the Northern Group, *Vincennes*, at the astounding range of nine miles. Per his battle plan, Mikawa headed north to attack the second group of enemy ships. Using the same tactic that crippled the Southern Group, the Japanese cruisers first attacked with torpedoes and then closed for a gun attack. At 0148hrs, *Chokai* launched four torpedoes at *Vincennes* from

six miles. Once again, the American ships were surprised. At 0150hrs, all three cruisers of the Northern Group were illuminated by powerful Japanese searchlights. With this illumination, the Japanese cruisers quickly found their targets. *Chokai* illuminated *Astoria* at 7,700 yards; *Aoba* found *Quincy* at 9,200 yards and *Kako* spotlighted *Vincennes* at 10,500 yards. The American ships were caught with their main guns trained fore and aft and the Japanese could see personnel running on their decks.

The skill and training of the Japanese cruiser gun crews was once again thoroughly displayed. *Aoba* and *Kako* scored hits on their third salvo and *Chokai* scored on her fifth. Heavy cruiser *Quincy* was quickly crippled, but the American ship went down fighting. *Aoba*'s early salvoes caused fires fed by *Quincy*'s floatplanes and also hit the ship's bridge. Soon, *Aoba*, *Furutaka* and *Tenryu* were pouring fire into *Quincy*. She managed to get off three salvoes against the Japanese before being forced out of action. *Aoba* and *Tenryu* added to the carnage with a total of three torpedo hits.

Light cruiser *Yubari* was commissioned in 1923 and carried a fairly heavy armament of six 5.5in. guns and four torpedo tubes on a small displacement of 2,890 tons. Despite her age, she played an important part of the Japanese victory at Savo Island. (Naval History and Heritage Command, 19-N-9957)

Heavy cruiser *Quincy* during the battle of Savo Island being illuminated by Japanese cruiser searchlights. *Quincy* was overwhelmed by accurate Japanese gunfire and then finished off by torpedoes. (Naval History and Heritage Command, NH 50346)

Heavy cruiser *Quincy* pictured on August 3, 1942 at New Caledonia before departing for the invasion of Guadalcanal. The cruiser was sunk days later by Japanese shells and torpedoes. Losses were very heavy, with 389 men killed and 147 wounded. (Naval History and Heritage Command, 80-G-K-563)

These, combined with 54 shell hits of various sizes, were enough to ensure *Quincy*'s destruction, with the loss of 370 of her crew. The cruiser was the first ship to sink during the battle, at 0238hrs, becoming the first ship of many to litter Iron Bottom Sound. In return, *Quincy* inflicted the only significant damage of the battle on the Japanese when she placed two 8in. rounds in the chartroom of *Chokai*'s bridge, barely missing Mikawa and his staff. Thirty-six men were killed or wounded.

Under fire from *Kako*, *Vincennes* quickly found a target for her 8in. guns and scored a hit on their second salvo, which damaged *Kinugasa*. *Kako* quickly began to score hits amidships which created a fire, again fed by the American cruiser's floatplanes. As *Vincennes*'s captain attempted radically to maneuver, one torpedo from *Chokai* hit at about 0155hrs. Another torpedo, this one from *Yubari*, hit at 0203hrs. *Chokai* continued to pummel the crippled cruiser and as many as 74 shells struck the vessel. The ship was abandoned at 0230hrs and she later sank at 0258hrs. A total of 332 crewmen were killed.

*Astoria*'s reaction to the sudden Japanese onslaught reflected the general confusion throughout the Northern Group. The ship's gunnery officer quickly ordered his 8in. guns to engage the enemy after his ship came under fire from *Chokai*, but the ship's skipper ordered his ship to cease fire after arriving on the bridge thinking that he was being fired upon by friendly ships. *Chokai*'s accurate fire knocked out two of *Astoria*'s three 8in. turrets, but *Astoria* was able to fire 53 8in. rounds before all her guns were knocked out. Gunfire from *Aoba*, *Kinugasa* and *Kako* finished off *Astoria* with between 34 and 63 hits. She sank with 216 of her crew.

The last action of the night occurred as the Japanese force was withdrawing to the north of Savo Island. At 0216hrs, *Tenryu* and *Furutaka* engaged

destroyer *Ralph Talbot*, still on patrol north of Savo Island. In the first exchange, the Japanese scored only a single hit. Minutes later, *Yubari* illuminated the destroyer and quickly scored five hits. *Ralph Talbot* was saved by a rain squall as the Japanese force continued its sweep to the northwest.

The Japanese retirement was the most controversial aspect of the battle. Having shattered Turner's covering force, Mikawa had the opportunity to turn a tactical victory into a strategic one. Little stood between him and the American transports. Off Tulagi were five transports screened by two destroyers and three destroyer transports, and off Guadalcanal were another 13 transports, escorted by another three destroyers and five old destroyer minesweepers. At 0216hrs, Mikawa analyzed the situation with his staff. As already mentioned, the Japanese force had split into two groups with destroyer *Yunagi* operating separately. The Japanese reckoned that it would take two hours to reassemble their force and reverse course to the east to attack the transports. This left only an hour of night and ensured that the force would be vulnerable to air attack when morning came. If Mikawa continued to track to the northwest, the Japanese would find themselves some 120 miles from Iron Bottom Sound and thus had a good chance of avoiding air attack from the carriers Mikawa assessed were rushing into position to deliver a morning attack. On the positive side for Mikawa, the engagement with the Allied cruiser forces still left the Japanese with around 60 percent of their gun ammunition and 50 percent of their torpedoes. After briefly considering his options, Mikawa decided at 0220hrs to break off the action and return to Rabaul.

Mikawa did not know it at the time, but he had just squandered the IJN's best chance of delivering a knockout blow to the first American offensive in the Pacific. It is hard to imagine the Americans holding on to their lodgment following the destruction of their transport fleet and the supplies still on board. The destruction of the American transports would have been worth the sacrifice of Mikawa's entire force.

### Savo Island: the aftermath

Though Mikawa's victorious battle was an incomplete triumph, Savo Island was still the worst US Navy defeat ever suffered at sea. When the *Canberra* sank at 0800hrs after being scuttled by American destroyers, this brought Allied losses to four heavy cruisers sunk and a fifth damaged. Two destroyers

Australian heavy cruiser *Canberra* the morning after the battle of Savo Island. The ship is listing to starboard and will soon sink. Alongside are American destroyers *Blue* and *Patterson* to remove the ship's survivors. (Naval History and Heritage Command, 80-G-13488)

were also damaged. Personnel losses were very heavy, with 1,077 sailors killed and 709 wounded.

Japanese losses were minor. *Chokai* suffered three hits that killed 34 and wounded 48. *Aoba* took topside damage but suffered no personnel casualties. *Kinugasa* had one killed and one wounded from two hits. The single 5in. hit on *Tenryu* killed 23 and wounded 21. The most severe loss was suffered after the battle on August 10 when American submarine *S-44* sank *Kako* on her way to Kavieng. The lack of a proper destroyer screen cost Mikawa in this instance. When *Kako* sank, 71 crewmen were killed and 15 wounded.

The battle of Savo Island confirmed several key facts. The IJN proved itself the master of night combat and established dominance in the waters around Guadalcanal at night. Japanese nightfighting doctrine proved itself under actual combat conditions and featured the use of superior night optics, the superb Type 93 torpedo and reliance on quick and accurate gunnery. Despite the fame of the Type 93 torpedo (and not all ships at Savo Island carried this weapon), it is important to note that Japanese gunfire was the primary agent of destruction at Savo Island.

Heavy cruiser *Chicago* anchored in Iron Bottom Sound the day after the battle of Savo Island. Sailors are cutting away damaged plating to enable the ship to get under way. The ship was struck by a single torpedo on her starboard side on the extreme forward part of her bow. The damage forced the ship out of action until early 1943. (Naval History and Heritage Command, 80-G-34685)

The submarine *S-44*, commissioned in 1925, achieved more than the entire Allied surface force during the battle for Savo Island when she torpedoed and sank Japanese heavy cruiser *Kako* on the morning of August 10, as the Japanese cruiser force was returning to its anchorage at Kavieng north of Rabaul. This was the most successful American submarine attack of the entire campaign. *S-44* survived the campaign, but was sunk in September 1943 in the North Pacific. (Naval History and Heritage Command, 19-N-41382)

For the Americans, there was little to view favorably. American nightfighting doctrine had been found wanting and American warships were simply not ready for night combat. The most important factor leading to the Savo Island debacle was the total surprise gained by the Japanese. This stemmed from command and control problems at every level, Turner's assessment of Japanese intentions, and his resulting faulty deployments. The potential technological advantage offered by radar was entirely squandered since commanders did not understand the capabilities and limitations of the new equipment.

## AUGUST AND SEPTEMBER INTERLUDE

Savo Island assured the Japanese control of the waters around Guadalcanal at night, but the presence of the American carrier force meant it was too dangerous for Japanese ships to operate during the day in the same waters. What developed was a strange situation in which control of the key waters around the island changed every time the sun went down. The Japanese immediately put their nocturnal advantage to use. On August 16, the first Japanese destroyers arrived at Tassafaronga Point with the first reinforcements for the Japanese garrison. This was followed on the night of August 18–19 when six destroyers delivered the first echelon of the Ichiki detachment. The attack by Colonel Ichiki and his battalion-sized unit on the eastern side of the Marine perimeter during the early hours of August 21 was repulsed with the near destruction of his entire unit. Not for the last time, the Japanese had thoroughly underestimated what it would take to wrest control of the island from the Marines.

As the Japanese were preparing for their first ground offensive to retake the island, on August 20 the first Marine aircraft arrived. The initial echelon was small – 19 F4F fighters and 12 SBD dive-bombers – but their arrival fundamentally changed the situation in the entire campaign. The waters around the island were now too dangerous for Japanese ships during the day, whether or not the American carriers were within range. Fundamentally, the struggle for the island was dictated by control of the airfield. If the Americans held it, they forced the Japanese to rely on inefficient destroyer transport to reinforce their garrison. Control of the waters during the day made possible regular resupply for the Marines. The Japanese quandary was clear – unless they could suppress the airfield, they could not move sufficient troops to the island to capture it. If they could not capture or neutralize the airfield, surface ships could not operate around the island to cut off the flow of American reinforcements.

Yamamoto was slow to react to the American offensive, but by late August he had assembled a considerable portion of the Combined Fleet to mount a major operation. This operation was centered on getting a small convoy to the island, carrying Ichiki's second echelon and some Special Naval Landing troops. Supporting the convoy was the rebuilt Japanese carrier force with three carriers. These had the critical mission of eliminating the American carrier force should it attempt to intervene. (See Campaign 247 *Santa Cruz 1942* for a detailed treatment of the carrier battles around Guadalcanal.)

The Japanese operation was poorly coordinated and failed to achieve either of its two primary objectives. The carrier battle on August 24, known as the battle of the Eastern Solomons, was indecisive. Aircraft from the carrier *Saratoga* sank the light Japanese carrier *Ryujo*. In return, the heavy Japanese carriers *Shokaku* and *Zuikaku* succeeded in damaging the carrier *Enterprise*. The next day, the Japanese convoy was attacked by American aircraft and lost one of its transports and a destroyer. The first major Japanese efforts to retake Guadalcanal, both on land and at sea, had failed.

Unable to move reinforcements to the island with slow transports vulnerable to air attack, the Japanese resorted to increasing the number of troops moving to Guadalcanal by destroyer. The next unit committed to recapture the island was the 35th Infantry Brigade. Each destroyer could carry only some 150 men and 30–40 tons of supplies, but timing their movement down "the Slot" could arrive at Guadalcanal during the night, unload, and then use their high speed to clear the island and get out of range of air attack by morning.

By early September, the lifeline provided by Japanese destroyers was in high gear. Occasionally, dive-bombers from Henderson Field would find the destroyers late in the evening or early the next morning, but these targets were very difficult to hit. The Americans made no move to impede these nocturnal operations with surface ships.

What few naval engagements there were during August and early September reinforced the Japanese sense of superiority in night combat. On August 22, a small destroyer action confirmed the verdict of Savo Island. Two American destroyers, *Blue* and *Henley*, were ordered into Iron Bottom Sound to protect a small convoy bringing supplies to the Marines. The Japanese had only a single destroyer, *Kawakaze*, to intercept. Though the American destroyers possessed radar, *Kawakaze* was able to get off the first shot and torpedoed *Blue* at 0359hrs. The Americans never got a shot off against the elusive Japanese destroyer and *Blue* was scuttled later that day.

A repeat performance was given on September 5 when three Japanese destroyers on a bombardment mission against Guadalcanal encountered two American destroyer transports, *Little* and *Gregory*. The American ships were World War I destroyers converted into transports, and carried only two 4in. guns and no torpedoes. The Japanese ships were all fleet destroyers and though totally surprised by the appearance of the two American ships, quickly turned their guns on the new contacts and made short work of both.

Using mainly destroyer runs, the Japanese moved an entire brigade to the island beginning in late August through September 7. The Americans made no attempt to interfere with these regular runs. The next Japanese ground

## The battle of Cape Esperance

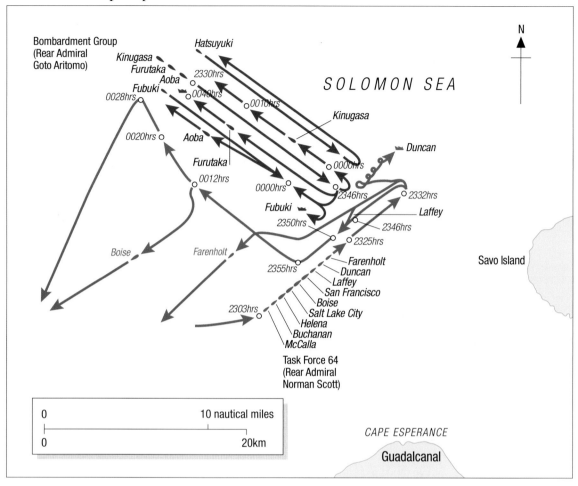

Bombardment Group (Rear Admiral Goto Aritomo)

SOLOMON SEA

Hatsuyuki
Kinugasa
Furutaka
Aoba
Fubuki
0028hrs
2330hrs
0040hrs
0010hrs
Kinugasa
0020hrs
Aoba
0000hrs
Furutaka
0012hrs
0000hrs
Duncan
2346hrs
2332hrs
Fubuki
2350hrs
Laffey
2346hrs
Boise
Farenholt
2325hrs
2355hrs
Farenholt
Duncan
Laffey
San Francisco
Boise
Salt Lake City
Helena
Buchanan
McCalla
2303hrs

Savo Island

Task Force 64 (Rear Admiral Norman Scott)

CAPE ESPERANCE

Guadalcanal

| 0 | 10 nautical miles |
|---|---|
| 0 | 20km |

assault was conducted by the 6,200 men of the 35th Infantry Brigade. The Japanese were facing a Marine garrison twice as large, but the Japanese did possess the element of surprise and the potential to mass overwhelming numbers at a single point along the Marine perimeter. The Japanese attack was finally launched on the night of September 12–13 against a thinly manned portion of the perimeter south of Henderson Field. The attack was poorly coordinated, and Marine firepower and tenacity crushed the attack with heavy losses. The outcome was that the Japanese finally realized that a more determined effort would be necessary to gain victory.

On September 15, a Japanese submarine sank the carrier *Wasp* and damaged the modern battleship *North Carolina* with a well-placed salvo of six torpedoes. This single action reduced the number of operational American carriers in the Pacific to one, making Ghormley even more reluctant to commit his carrier force. With *North Carolina* out of action, only two fast battleships were available for operations off Guadalcanal. On September 18 the Marine garrison on the island received some good news when Turner ordered a convoy through to land the 7th Marine Regiment.

Ghormley finally decided that he had to contest the continuing Japanese reinforcement runs to the island. On September 20, he created Task Force 64

HMAS *Australia* under way as the Allied task force leaves the waters around Guadalcanal on August 9 after the disaster at the battle of Savo Island. *Australia* was the flagship of Allied forces in the battle, but saw no action. *Australia* and *Canberra* were both County-class heavy cruisers built in Great Britain and armed with eight 8in. guns, but with a generally inadequate level of protection. (Naval History and Heritage Command, 80-G-13492)

and initially assigned it three cruisers and some seven destroyers under the command of Rear Admiral Scott. This move was none too soon and coincided with the Japanese decision to up the ante on Guadalcanal by sending in the 2nd Infantry Division and parts of the 38th Infantry Division. These 17,500 men, they judged, should be sufficient to crush the Marines.

# THE BATTLE OF CAPE ESPERANCE

Scott had two missions for his new command. First, he had the responsibility of getting the convoy carrying the 164th Infantry Regiment of the Americal Division to Guadalcanal. This was accomplished on October 13. More importantly, his force of four cruisers and five destroyers had orders to prevent any Japanese reinforcement of the island or to stop any attempt to bombard Henderson Field.

## BATTLE OF CAPE ESPERANCE ORDER OF BATTLE

**UNITED STATES NAVY**

| | |
|---|---|
| Task Force 64 | Rear Admiral Norman Scott |

Heavy cruisers *Salt Lake City, San Francisco*
Light cruisers *Boise, Helena*
Destroyers *Buchanan, Duncan, Farenholt, Laffey, McCalla*

**IMPERIAL JAPANESE NAVY**

| | |
|---|---|
| Bombardment Group | Rear Admiral Goto Aritomo |

Heavy cruisers *Aoba, Furutaka, Kinugasa*
Destroyers *Fubuki, Hatsuyuki*
Reinforcement Group
Seaplane tenders *Chitose, Nisshin*
Destroyers *Asagumo, Natsugumo, Yamagumo, Murakumo, Shirayuki, Akizuki*

Scott had attempted to incorporate some of the lessons learned at Savo Island while formulating his battle plan. He was handicapped by the scratch nature of his command and the continuing proclivity of American naval commanders to dismiss the offensive potential of their destroyers. The tactics he devised reflect both these realities. Scott opted for a simple column formation with destroyers deployed ahead and astern of the four cruisers. The destroyers were ordered to illuminate targets with star shells after gaining radar contact.

He did make provisions for destroyers to use their torpedoes against large targets and to engage smaller targets with their 5in. guns. The centerpiece of Scott's plan was to use his cruiser gunnery to decimate the Japanese. Scott wanted his cruisers to engage as soon they had a target and intended to use the cruiser floatplanes for target illumination. Placing his destroyers at the front and end of his formation gave the cruisers clear fields of fire and reduced the problem of identifying friend from foe, always a difficult feat at night.

Scott's tactics for the upcoming battle were an intelligent attempt to make up for the lack of a proven nightfighting doctrine. However, Scott's plan did have several flaws. The first of these was the aforementioned negligence to the offensive use of his destroyers. He also did not maximize the use of his biggest potential advantage – radar. While his two heavy cruisers both carried radar, these were the unreliable and short-ranged SC version. His two light cruisers carried the much superior SG radar. Sticking to tradition, Scott selected one of the heavy cruisers as his flagship. This unfortunate choice had great ramifications in the battle. Scott was also unaware of the true capabilities of the Japanese Type 93 long-range torpedo, so his assumption that cruiser gunnery would out-range Japanese torpedoes was another fundamental flaw. He did make allowances for Japanese torpedo tactics by planning to break his force into smaller sections if the torpedo threat was assessed to be significant. To be fair to Scott in this regard, no other American admiral showed true respect for the Type 93 until well after the Guadalcanal campaign.

Following the formation of Task Force 64 on September 20, Scott had the opportunity to run his command through several battle drills. He did not have to wait long to see if his tactics worked. On October 9 and 10, he lingered south of Guadalcanal but did not receive word of any Japanese activity. On October 11, a B-17 sighted the Japanese Reinforcement Group heading to the island, but the Bombardment Group was not sighted. The reported contact was due to arrive at the northwest tip of Guadalcanal at 2300hrs on the 11th.

Scott's pre-battle intelligence was correct – the Japanese did plan a major operation for the night of October 11–12. A reinforcement group with two high-speed seaplane carriers carrying artillery and five destroyers loaded with troops (a sixth carried no troops) were on their way to the island. Trailing behind was a bombardment group of three cruisers and two destroyers under the command of Rear Admiral Goto Aritomo. The cruisers were loaded with specially fused shells designed to cause maximum destruction of aircraft and personnel on Henderson Field. The fact that the Reinforcement Group preceded the Bombardment Group was evidence that the Japanese expected no challenge from the Americans.

## The battle opens

As Scott reached a point west of Savo Island, American technology began to weigh in. The SG radar aboard light cruiser *Helena* picked up a contact at 27,700 yards at 2325hrs. This contact was not reported to Scott. Unaware that action was pending, Scott ordered his ships to reverse course at 2332hrs. The movement was not executed smartly, with some of the cruisers executing an immediate turn instead of the entire column pivoting on a single point and maintaining formation. The net effect was that Scott's column was thrown into confusion with the three lead destroyers moving to the starboard flank

**THE BATTLE OF CAPE ESPERANCE (pp. 50–51)**

*Furutaka* **(1)** was the first Japanese heavy cruiser sunk in a surface action during the war. She was part of Rear Admiral Goto's Bombardment Force which was headed into Iron Bottom Sound on the night of October 11–12 to conduct the first bombardment of Henderson Field by heavy naval guns. For the first time since the battle of Savo Island, the Americans decided to contest the nighttime waters around Guadalcanal. A task force under Rear Admiral Scott had the mission of stopping the bombardment. The Americans gained first contact with radar, but largely squandered this advantage by not immediately opening fire. Nevertheless, when they did open fire, the gained complete surprise and began to pummel the unsuspecting Japanese. *Furutaka* is shown in this view under heavy fire. During the battle, she took some 90 hits from American 8-, 6- and 5-in. shells, as well possibly as a single torpedo, which caused fires **(2)**, knocked out her armament, and eventually brought her to a halt. Her response against Scott's ships was ineffective. During the morning of October 12, the ship sank due to progressive flooding; 258 of her crew were killed in this action. This encounter, named the battle of Cape Esperance, was the first time during the war that the IJN lost a night battle.

of the cruisers. Unfortunately for Scott, the battle broke out as the three destroyers were racing down the starboard side of the cruisers to take their designated place in the front of the formation.

A key part of Scott's battle plan was the expectation that the cruisers would open fire when they gained contact. Despite these standing orders, *Helena* continued to track the Japanese on radar without taking action. The movement of the lead American destroyers probably increased the hesitation to open fire. At 2345hrs, the range had closed to only 3,600 yards and the approaching Japanese were visible to American lookouts. Finally, at 2346hrs following a confusing exchange with Scott, the captain of the *Helena* gave orders to open fire. Scott, aboard heavy cruiser *San Francisco*, which did not have SG radar, never had a clear picture of the battle area and remained concerned about the location of his destroyers.

As Scott struggled to piece together the contact reports that were flooding in, Goto refused to believe that he was about to be challenged by the Americans at night. When he received a report at 2343hrs of three ships at 11,000 yards, Goto ordered that recognition lights be flashed to the contacts, which he assumed to be the Reinforcement Group. Even after his lookouts identified the contacts as American ships, Goto failed to act. Just as the Japanese had gained surprise at Savo Island, at Cape Esperance they lost it, and now they were about to pay the price.

Following their turn and in spite of the opening confusion, Scott's force began the action in a very favorable tactical situation. After their turn, the American cruisers were steaming on a southwesterly course, which meant they were "capping the T" of Goto's force. While the American cruisers could employ their entire broadside, the Japanese could reply only with their forward guns. The lead ship in Goto's formation was his flagship, heavy cruiser *Aoba*. *Boise*, both heavy cruisers and a destroyer took *Aoba* under fire which knocked out the Japanese cruiser's two forward 8in. turrets, destroyed her fire control equipment and killed Goto on his bridge. As gunfire rained down on the surprised Japanese, their formation broke up. *Aoba*, *Furutaka* and a destroyer made a turn to starboard. *Kinugasa* and *Hatsuyuki* turned to port, which almost certainly saved them from destruction.

*Furutaka* was a member of the first class of Japanese heavy cruisers. She displaced 8,100 tons and carried six 8in. guns and eight 24in. torpedo tubes. After being victorious at Savo Island, *Furutaka* was sunk at the battle of Cape Esperance. (Yamato Museum, 070337)

Hatsuyuki was another Special Type destroyer. She participated in the battle of Cape Esperance and the Second Naval Battle of Guadalcanal, surviving both. She was sunk by aircraft in July 1943 while on a transport run from Rabaul. (Yamato Museum, 064113)

Aoba was the only member of Sentai 6 to survive the Guadalcanal campaign. She fought into 1944, was damaged at the battle of Leyte Gulf and was finally sunk by air attack at Kure, Japan, in July 1945. (Yamato Museum, 070223)

Convinced his ships were firing on his own destroyers, Scott ordered a largely ignored ceasefire at 2347hrs. Four minutes later, Scott rescinded his order after he assessed that his targets were all Japanese. However, by this time two of his van destroyers had already been struck by 6in. American shells, confirming Scott's fears. The second destroyer in line, *Duncan*, made radar contact on the Japanese after she executed her turn at the start of the battle. Her captain immediately changed course toward the contact, which was four miles away. This placed her between the two sides when the battle opened. Only 1,000 yards away from the Japanese force, *Duncan* was engaged by the enemy and radar-directed 6in. gunfire from *Helena*. In response, she fired five torpedoes at *Furutaka*. According to the Japanese, one of these hit the cruiser at 2358hrs making it one of the few American destroyer torpedo successes of the entire campaign. *Duncan* was set afire, forcing the crew to abandon ship; the destroyer sank the next day. *Farenholt* was also struck by American 6in. gunfire and suffered three dead and 40 wounded. The destroyer was forced to withdraw. The last destroyer in the van group, *Laffey*, was undamaged and she moved to a position of relative safety in the rear of the American column.

Under a barrage of gunfire, the Japanese formation broke into two groups and headed to the northwest. *Aoba* responded feebly with seven rounds from her undamaged aft 8in. turret. *Furutaka* was able to return fire with 30 8in.

shells before being struck by many shells that destroyed her aft 8in. turret and hit her torpedo launchers, which created a large fire. The cruiser was also struck in two of her engine rooms, but was able to continue to the northwest. Destroyer *Fubuki* came under fire from *Boise* and *San Francisco* and quickly exploded and sank.

## Cape Esperance: phase two

At 2353hrs, Scott turned the remaining ships he still had control over – four cruisers and destroyers *Buchanan* and *McCalla* – to the northwest to pursue the fleeing Japanese. The Americans concentrated their gunnery on *Aoba* and *Furutaka*. *Furutaka* took some 90 hits, which eventually brought the cruiser to a halt and she sank later that morning, owing to flooding caused by numerous hits below the waterline. *Aoba* was struck by over 40 shells, but her watertight integrity was not threatened and she was able to depart the area at high speed. The outstanding performance of *Kinugasa* demonstrated the excellence of individual Japanese units. When the American barrage began, she turned to port and escaped the devastation that befell the rest of Goto's command. Around midnight, *Kinugasa* reentered the fight by engaging *San Francisco* with gunfire and then launching torpedoes at *Boise*. When *Boise* unwisely employed her searchlights, *Kinugasa* took her under fire with 8in. shells and quickly scored. The first hit was on *Boise*'s forward

Destroyer *Buchanan* refueling from carrier *Wasp* on August 3, en route to Guadalcanal. The ship is in its striking Measure 12 (modified) camouflage scheme. *Buchanan* was a Benson-class unit and was present at Savo Island, but saw no action and fought in the Battle of Cape Esperance. *Buchanan* received 16 battle stars and a Presidential Unit citation, making her one of the most decorated American warships of the Pacific War. (Naval History and Heritage Command, 80-G-K-420)

barbette and this was followed by an 8in. hit below the waterline that entered the cruiser's forward magazine and started a severe fire. Before the war, the Japanese designed what they called "diving shells" to penetrate below the waterline. This was the only known instance during the entire war where the diving shells performed as designed. The hit was nearly fatal, but the hole created by the shell caused the magazine to flood and saved the cruiser from destruction. *Kinugasa* followed up this virtuoso performance by scoring at least two hits on *Salt Lake City*, which had also used her searchlights and revealed her position. The first pierced the cruiser's weak armor belt and caused minor flooding, but the second created a major fire and resulted in loss of steering. In exchange, *Kinugasa* suffered minor damage from four hits. Scott terminated the pursuit of the Japanese at 0028hrs on October 12, bringing the battle to a close.

### Cape Esperance: the reckoning

The Japanese had lost their first night action of the war in convincing fashion. Of the three Japanese cruisers present, *Furutaka* was sunk with 258 of her crew killed, *Aoba* was heavily damaged and had to return to Japan for repairs (she returned to action in January 1943), and only *Kinugasa* survived in condition to fight again. Of the two destroyers, *Fubuki* was sunk with some 78 killed (unusually, the remainder of her crew, 111 men, was taken prisoner) and *Hatsuyuki* suffered minor damage. The only good fortune for the Japanese was that the Reinforcement Group completed its mission.

Though they were victorious, the Americans still paid a steep price. The only ship sunk was the destroyer *Duncan* which was struck by shells from both sides and suffered 48 killed and 35 wounded. The damage to *Boise* was severe and another 107 were killed and 29 wounded. *Salt Lake City* was less severely damaged but still required six months' work to repair. Damage to destroyer *Farenholt*, again by "friendly" fire, forced her to return to the United States for repairs.

Cape Esperance was the first battle where radar played an important role. Scott's indecision and the refusal of *Helena*'s captain to open fire after gaining inital contact largely squandered the advantage provided by radar, but the Japanese had still been surprised and suffered accordingly. The victory showed that the Japanese could be defeated at night, but lost in the victory was the fact that American losses were also high and that they would not again challenge the Japanese at night for another month. An unfortunate side effect for the Americans was that Scott's tactics were judged to be good and were used in the next night battle with less then desirable results.

What generally goes unmentioned in the aftermath of Cape Esperance is that the Japanese continued to command the nighttime seas around Guadalcanal. Goto's abortive

The most heavily damaged American cruiser at the battle of Cape Esperance was *Boise*. She suffered eight shell hits during the battle, the most serious of which penetrated the ship under water and started a fire in the forward magazine. This view, taken at the Philadelphia Navy Yard in November 1942, shows a hit on the face of the forward triple 6in. turret that failed to penetrate the 6.5in. turret face armor. (Naval History and Heritage Command, 80-G-300232)

Destroyer *Duncan* on October 7, 1942. *Duncan* was the only American ship sunk during the battle of Cape Esperance when she was caught between the opposing task forces and targeted by gunfire from both sides. Forty-eight of her crew died in this engagement. This was not the last occasion on which American sailors fired on their own ships. (Naval History and Heritage Command, NH-90495)

bombardment was a single part in a much bigger operation. The centerpiece of the Japanese plan was the movement to the island of a "High-Speed Convoy" of six fast transports escorted by eight destroyers. These ships carried 4,500 troops, some artillery and much-needed supplies. To ensure the convoy made it intact, Yamamoto unveiled a surprise. A task force led by battleships *Kongo* and *Haruna*, escorted by a light cruiser and nine destroyers, was ordered to saturate the airfield with 14in. shells. Against opposition offered by only four tardy American torpedo boats, the battleships began their methodical bombardment at 0033hrs on October 14. The effect of the shelling, which included special Type 3 incendiary shells, was devastating. By the time the bombardment concluded at 0156hrs, the two battleships had delivered a total of 973 14in. shells, making Henderson Field unusable and accounting for half of the aircraft present and most of the aviation fuel.

By midnight on October 14, the six transports arrived at Guadalcanal intact. All of their troops were landed and most of their supplies. Three of the ships were sunk by aircraft from a resurgent Henderson Field. In reply, Yamamoto ordered another heavy cruiser bombardment of the airfield on the night of October 15–16. The American position at sea looked bleak, but on land, when the newly arrived Japanese troops launched their attack on October 24–25, they were again repulsed.

### The Americans change command

With intelligence indicating that another major Japanese effort was pending, Ghormley grew more pessimistic about whether Guadalcanal could be held. On October 15 he send a message to Nimitz describing his forces as "totally inadequate" to meet the next Japanese offensive. Having made a visit to the South Pacific from September 30 to October 2, Nimitz knew that the pessimism so prevalent at Ghormley's headquarters at Noumea was not shared on Guadalcanal itself. Feeling that morale needed a boost and more aggressive leadership was required to support the Marines, Nimitz made the choice, approved by King, to replace Ghormley with Halsey, who was already in the South Pacific for familiarization before taking over command of the carrier task force. Immediately after assuming command of the South Pacific on October 18, Halsey promised the Marines he would provide them with all possible support. This translated into a major carrier battle in late October and two major surface battles in November.

The battle of Santa Cruz, fought on October 26, 1942, essentially removed both the American and Japanese carrier forces from further large-scale participation in the campaign. Of the two American carriers present, *Hornet* was sunk and *Enterprise*, shown here under attack, was damaged. Of the four Japanese carriers engaged, two were damaged and forced to return to Japan for repairs. Yamamoto was sure he had sunk three American carriers, which led him to believe the American carriers would not factor further into the battle. (Naval History and Heritage Command, 80-G-20989)

# THE FIRST NAVAL BATTLE OF GUADALCANAL

The battle of Santa Cruz, fought between the carrier forces on October 26, had been a resounding defeat for the American carrier force and Yamamoto no longer believed it would be a factor in the campaign. Now, all that was left to do was suppress Henderson Field in order to move sufficient troops to the island finally to crush the Marines. The number required would far surpass the ability of just destroyer transport runs alone. Destroyers succeeded in delivering some 8,000 troops of the 38th Division between October 23 and November 11, but to move the division's heavy equipment, a convoy would be required. To accomplish this, the Japanese organized a convoy of 11 fast transport ships, which were scheduled to arrive on the island on November 14.

Preceding the arrival of the convoy, the Combined Fleet had ordered a repeat of the successful October battleship bombardment against Henderson Field. This was part of a massive operation in which the convoy was escorted by 12 destroyers and supported by the 8th Fleet with its four heavy cruisers, one light cruiser and six destroyers. The Combined Fleet departed Truk with a single carrier, four battleships, three heavy cruisers, three light cruisers and 21 destroyers.

# The First Naval Battle of Guadalcanal

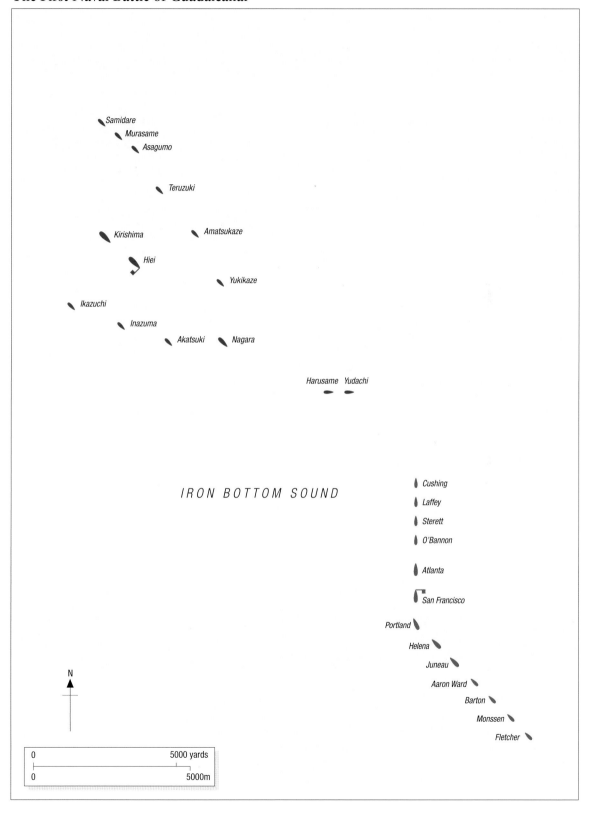

Samidare

Murasame

Asagumo

Teruzuki

Kirishima

Amatsukaze

Hiei

Yukikaze

Ikazuchi

Inazuma

Akatsuki   Nagara

Harusame  Yudachi

IRON BOTTOM SOUND

Cushing

Laffey

Sterett

O'Bannon

Atlanta

San Francisco

Portland

Helena

Juneau

Aaron Ward

Barton

Monssen

Fletcher

N

0                    5000 yards

0                    5000m

Such a major operation could not escape the notice of American intelligence. Halsey knew a major Japanese operation was under way and that it included a major troop convoy to Guadalcanal. Both he and Turner suspected that the Japanese would attempt a repeat of their October bombardment. To contend with the Japanese offensive, Halsey had two major forces. The carrier *Enterprise*, damaged at Santa Cruz, formed the center of a task force with two fast battleships, a heavy cruiser, a light antiaircraft cruiser and eight destroyers. As the timing of the Japanese move unfolded, this task force was too far from Guadalcanal to interfere with the initial Japanese assault. The only ships available to stop the expected bombardment were the escort to an American convoy which had arrived at Guadalcanal and the cruiser-destroyer force created by Ghormley before the battle of Cape Esperance. Together, this amounted to two heavy cruisers, one light cruiser, two light antiaircraft cruisers, and eight destroyers. The combined force was placed under the command of Rear Admiral Callaghan, who replaced Scott.

The American task force was active in Iron Bottom Sound on the night of November 11–12, but the Japanese were not present. Callaghan was informed that the Japanese would be present in force the next night. His orders from Turner were to prevent a bombardment of the airfield. He was under no illusion about the difficulty of his mission. After escorting the transports out of Iron Bottom Sound, he turned his force back to meet the Japanese. As Scott had done at Cape Esperance, he deployed his force in a line-ahead formation. Four destroyers led the column with the five cruisers in the center, followed up by the other four destroyers.

The Japanese force assigned to conduct the bombardment was commanded by Rear Admiral Abe. He did not expect the Americans to be present after dark, but he was taking no chances. He detailed one of his destroyer squadrons with five destroyers to scout ahead of his main body, which included his two battleships escorted by another destroyer squadron with a light cruiser and six destroyers. During the run to the island, Abe's force had encountered poor weather, which included very heavy thunderstorms, bringing visibility down to zero. At 0005hrs on November 13, he ordered a 180-degree turn to get out of the bad weather. This was followed by another 180-degree turn at 0038hrs after the weather had cleared. The net effect of the poor weather on the approach and the enforced maneuvering was to disperse the Japanese formation and make it vulnerable to surprise.

# FIRST NAVAL BATTLE OF GUADALCANAL
# ORDER OF BATTLE

## UNITED STATES NAVY

Task Force 67                 Rear Admiral Daniel Callaghan on *San Francisco*

    Heavy cruisers *San Francisco, Portland*

    Light cruisers *Helena, Atlanta, Juneau*

    Destroyers (Van) *Cushing, Laffey, Sterett, O'Bannon* (Rear) *Aaron Ward, Barton,*
       *Monssen, Fletcher*

## IMPERIAL JAPANESE NAVY

Bombardment Group          Vice Admiral Abe Hiroaki on *Hiei*

    Sentai 11

       Battleships *Hiei, Kirishima*

    Destroyer Squadron 10      Rear Admiral Kimura Satsuma on *Nagara*

       Light cruiser *Nagara*

       Destroyer Division 6 *Akatsuki, Ikazuchi, Inazuma*

       Destroyer Division 16 *Amatsukaze, Yukikaze*

       Destroyer Division 61 *Teruzuki*

Sweeping Unit

    (Destroyer Squadron 4)      Rear Admiral Takama Tamotsu on *Asagumo*

       Destroyer Division 2 *Harusame, Murasame, Samidare, Yudachi*

Patrol Unit (assigned to cover the area between Guadalcanal and the Russell Islands,
    and did not see action)

       Destroyer Division 27 *Shigure, Shiratsuyu, Yugure*

## *The most vicious night battle of the war*

Instead of having his destroyers 8,750 yards ahead of his battleships as planned, only two of Abe's five lead destroyers were in the proper position, and these were only a few thousand yards in advance of his main body. The other three destroyers of the lead destroyer squadron were actually behind his battleships. Abe knew nothing of this. Since he had heard nothing from his scouts, he decided to commence the bombardment at 0138hrs. Accordingly, the battleships began loading the Type 3 high-explosive shell filled with incendiaries. These were not suited for engaging warships.

As Abe was deciding that the coast was clear, Callaghan had already received information on the approaching Japanese. The SG radar on *Helena* detected the Japanese at 0124hrs. The lead Japanese destroyer was picked up at 27,000 yards and the battleships at 32,000 yards. Minutes later, at 0128hrs, Callaghan ordered a course change to the northwest, directly at the oncoming Japanese. Subsequently, he planned to come to starboard to cross the T of the Japanese. At 0137hrs, Callaghan ordered his lead ship, the destroyer *Cushing*, to head directly north. Within minutes, at 0141hrs, *Cushing* spotted ships crossing her bow and turned to the left to bring her guns and torpedoes to bear. The ships spotted by *Cushing* were the lead Japanese destroyers, *Yudachi* and *Harusame*. As Callaghan tried to make sense out of *Cushing*'s report and the increasing number of radar reports from other SG radar-equipped ships, he did alert his command at 0145hrs to be ready to fire.

**THE FIRST BATTLE OF GUADALCANAL (pp. 62–63)**

On the night of November 12–13, a large Japanese task force including two battleships was headed toward Guadalcanal to conduct a bombardment of Henderson Field. In order to save the airfield from devastation, the Americans were forced to intercept the Japanese with a smaller force of cruisers and destroyers. Both sides closed until the formations were almost intermingled. At 0148hrs, the lead Japanese battleship, *Hiei*, used her searchlights to illuminate targets for the rest of the fleet **(1)**. These lights settled on the lead American cruiser, *Atlanta* **(2)**. At a range of only 1,600 yards, *Atlanta* fired the first shots of the battle to take out the lights on *Hiei*. This scene shows the opening moments of the most vicious night battle of the war. Both *Atlanta* and *Hiei* would be severely damaged during this encounter. *Atlanta* could not be salvaged and sank later that afternoon. *Hiei* came under concerted American air attack and also sank, the first Japanese battleship to sink during the war. The cost of battle was high for

both sides. Of the 13 American ships engaged, only two destroyers emerged undamaged. Of the five cruisers, *Atlanta* was sunk, *Juneau* heavily damaged and sunk later in the day by submarine attack, heavy cruisers *San Francisco* and *Portland* were heavily damaged, and light cruiser *Helena* suffered moderate damage. Four of the eight destroyers involved were sunk (*Cushing*, *Laffey*, *Monssen* and *Barton*, and another two heavily damaged. Seven of the 14 Japanese ships engaged were damaged or sunk. *Hiei*'s fate has already been mentioned, and destroyers *Akatsuki* and *Yudachi* were also sunk. Two destroyers were heavily damaged and another two suffered light damage. Though the cost was high for the US Navy, the Japanese bombardment failed which led to the destruction of the large convoy headed to Guadalcanal and the ultimate failure of the last Japanese attempt to retake the island.

Light cruiser *Atlanta*, shown here on October 25, 1942 in the South Pacific, was a capable anti aircraft ship with her battery of 16 5in. dual-purpose guns, but her light armor made her ill-suited for a surface engagement. As the lead cruiser in the American column in the First Naval Battle of Guadalcanal, she was taken under fire by both sides and also hit by a Type 93 torpedo. She sank the next evening off Lunga Point; 170 men of her crew were lost. (Naval History and Heritage Command, 80-G-266844)

Callaghan's hesitation meant he lost control of the battle and forced his command into a close-range free-for-all. *Yudachi* had spotted *Cushing* and issued a warning to Abe. Lookouts on Abe's flagship, *Hiei*, spotted enemy ships at 10,000 yards. Abe ordered *Hiei* to use her searchlights to illuminate the American force, and light cruiser *Nagara* and destroyer *Akatsuki* followed suit. The lead American cruiser, *Atlanta*, attracted this unwanted attention and in response her captain ordered his forward batteries to engage the source of the light. The time was 0150hrs.

This first gunfire opened what was the most vicious, close-quarter night engagement of the war. Twenty-seven ships found themselves engaged in a life-and-death struggle. The details of this action are hard to reconstruct, and will never be fully and accurately known.

The ships in the van of each formation were immediately caught up in a maelstrom of gunfire. One of the most heavily engaged was *Atlanta*. Since she was the biggest object immediately available, a number of Japanese ships selected her as a target. At least *Hiei*, *Nagara*, *Inazuma* and *Ikazuchi* sent shells at the cruiser, which was still illuminated by searchlights. In the span of only a couple of minutes, the cruiser took some 32 hits. Minutes later, the burning *Atlanta* came under fire from *San Francisco*, the next cruiser in line behind *Atlanta*. Unfortunately, *San Francisco* shot accurately, scoring 19 8in. hits on *Atlanta*. Among those killed was Admiral Scott. Following this barrage, one of the 12 torpedoes launched from *Inazuma* and *Ikazuchi* found *Atlanta* at 0153hrs. The torpedo hit on her port side in the forward engine room and soon primary power was lost. *Atlanta* survived the night, but the flooding could not be contained, and the cruiser finally succumbed off Lunga Point at 2015hrs the next night. Of her crew of some 670 men, 172 were killed and another 79 wounded.

*Akatsuki* was a member of the last group of Special Type destroyers. She participated in the First Naval Battle of Guadalcanal during which she was quickly overwhelmed by American gunfire after unwisely using her searchlights. *Akatsuki* was apparently unable to employ her torpedoes in the battle, and was sunk with heavy loss of life. (Yamato Museum, 071774)

Destroyer *Cushing* was a Mahan-class unit that fought at the battle of Santa Cruz in October and was then assigned to Callaghan's force before the Second Naval Battle of Guadalcanal. As the lead ship in the American column, she was quickly targeted by ships from both sides and struck by shells at least ten times. Her burning hulk sank the next afternoon with 72 of her crew dead or missing. This is *Cushing* on July 15, before the battle. (Naval History and Heritage Command, NH 97852)

Destroyer *Laffey*, shown here packed with survivors from carrier *Wasp* after the latter had been torpedoed on September 15, was the second ship in the American column at the First Naval Battle of Guadalcanal. She began the battle by engaging *Akatsuki* with 5in. gunfire, and then shifted fire to battleship *Hiei*. Two of her torpedoes bounced off the battleship's hull because they had been launched too close to arm. Her 5in. turrets raked the battleship's superstructure, causing damage and personnel casualties. After avoiding a collision with *Hiei*, *Laffey* was engaged by three Japanese destroyers and battleship *Kirishima*, and then finished off by a Type 93 torpedo. For her fearless performance, *Laffey* earned a Presidential Unit Citation. (Naval History and Heritage Command, NH 97865)

Before being knocked out of the fight, *Atlanta* was able to land blows against the Japanese. She was actually the first ship to open fire when at 0150hrs, her fast-firing 5in. mounts took *Hiei* under fire. Other mounts aboard *Atlanta* engaged *Akatsuki*, the lead destroyer in Abe's starboard destroyer group and a visible target since she was using her searchlights on *Atlanta*. *Helena* joined in with her 6in. guns and *San Francisco* added to the deluge with her 8in. guns. *Akatsuki* was shattered by gunfire, knocked out of action, and shortly thereafter sank by the stern. Of her crew of some 200, there were only 18 survivors.

As the lead Japanese battleship and the biggest target, *Hiei* received the most attention from the Americans. The lead two American destroyers, *Cushing* and *Laffey* each engaged *Hiei* with torpedoes and gunfire. *Cushing* fired a single torpedo and raked the battleship's looming superstructure with 20mm fire. *Laffey* opened fire against *Hiei*'s pagoda superstructure with her 5in. main battery and smaller automatic weapons. She also fired five torpedoes at the battleship, but none hit or was able to arm at such a short distance. *Laffey* barely missed being rammed by *Hiei* and was so close the Japanese could not depress their guns far enough to engage the American ship. At such short range, the Americans hit their target with devastating effect. Abe and the *Hiei*'s captain were both wounded and Abe's chief of staff killed. The next destroyer, *Sterett* also hit the battleship with many 5in. shells, and launched four more torpedoes at the battleship, without success. In return, *Sterett* was engaged by Japanese destroyer gunfire and knocked out in action. Destroyer *Aaron Ward* directed ten 5in. gun salvoes at the battleship.

By 0156hrs, several levels of *Hiei*'s superstructure were aflame. The two American heavy cruisers, *San Francisco* and *Portland*, both selected the well-armored *Hiei* as their target. At one point, the two flagships, *Hiei* and *San Francisco*, were only 2,500 yards apart as they blasted away at each other. Both ships scored hits, but the Type 3 incendiary shells fired by *Hiei* failed to penetrate the cruiser's armor. A total of between 28 and 38 8in. shells were estimated to have struck *Hiei* during the battle, but the most

important, probably from *San Francisco*, struck the battleship at about 0154hrs on her starboard quarter and created a large hole in the hull. Significant amounts of water entered the ship as she maneuvered at high speed. The water entered the generator room, shorted it out, and as a result *Hiei* lost steering power. The captain switched to manual steering, and the ship was able to complete a turn to the north. Topside, the ship was in shambles from the 8in. shells and an estimated 70–74 5in. shells. With electrical power largely out and fire control equipment knocked out, the battleship's primary and secondary guns were useless. However, since the damage was largely confined to above the waterline, and the ship was still able to make 10 knots, the Japanese had reason to believe *Hiei* would survive as she limped north out of the battle.

*Hiei* was able to deal punishing blows before she was forced out of the fight. Her 14in. and 6in. secondary batteries took *San Francisco* under fire and her main battery scored three hits on its third salvo. The cruiser's superstructure was shattered and casualties were heavy. Admiral Callaghan and the *San Francisco*'s captain were killed; both were awarded posthumous Medals of Honor.

The lead American destroyer group also suffered heavily. *Cushing* was taken under fire by light cruiser *Nagara*'s 5.5in. guns, and the veteran cruiser scored numerous hits, destroying *Cushing*'s guns and steering and leaving her without power. Minutes later, destroyers *Asagumo* and *Marusame* came across the crippled American destroyer as they belatedly joined the battle, and scored additional hits. *Cushing*'s skipper ordered the remaining crew to abandon ship. The ship sank with a loss of 59 killed and 56 wounded.

Behind *Cushing* was destroyer *Laffey*. After engaging *Hiei* at short range, at least three Japanese destroyers, *Asagumo*, *Marusame* and *Samidare*, combined their 5in. gunfire against *Laffey* and scored many hits. A torpedo, probably from *Asagumo*, hit *Laffey* aft and left the ship without propulsive power. A 14in. hit,

Benson-class destroyer *Monssen*, shown here in May 1942 with carrier *Enterprise*, spent the first phase of the Guadalcanal campaign assigned to carrier screening duties. Present at the First Naval Battle of Guadalcanal, she was pummeled by almost 40 shells and sank the next afternoon with the loss of 145 men of her crew. (Naval History and Heritage Command, NH 97817)

probably from *Hiei*, finished off the destroyer. Loss of life was very heavy, and included her captain.

After nearly colliding with the lead American destroyer at the start of the action, destroyer *Yudachi* had veered to port. At 0158hrs, *Yudachi* gained a solution against the American cruisers and fired a full torpedo salvo. One of these hit *Portland* on her starboard side aft, destroying the two starboard shafts and jamming her rudder in a starboard turn. The cruiser circled helplessly for the remainder of the action, but was able to fire four salvoes from her forward two turrets against *Hiei*.

Destroyer *Amatsukaze* with her aggressive captain, jumped into the fray at 0154hrs with a full salvo of eight torpedoes. Their target was the rear group of four American destroyers. The lead Japanese destroyer, *Yudachi*, had cut in front of this column of four destroyers. *Aaron Ward* swerved to avoid a collision with the Japanese ship, and the next destroyer, *Barton*, had to stop to avoid a collision with *Aaron Ward*. Two of *Amatsukaze*'s torpedoes hit the stopped *Barton*, which quickly broke in two and sank at 0159hrs with the loss of all but 42 of her crew. In the span of less than ten minutes, two Japanese and six American ships had been sunk, were in the process of sinking, or were heavily damaged. At 0200hrs, the wounded Abe was forced to cancel the bombardment mission. He ordered a withdrawal to a position north of Savo Island. *Nagara* stood by the wounded *Hiei*, but Abe ordered *Kirishima*, which had taken only a single 8in. hit that caused little damage, to clear the area.

Despite the fact that the Americans had fulfilled their mission of stopping the bombardment, and Abe had ordered a withdrawal, the deadly close-range combat between the intermingled warships continued. As *Amatsukaze* engaged *San Francisco*, *Helena* brought the destroyer under fire and knocked out her main guns and steering. *Amatsukaze*, with 43 dead crewmen, was forced to leave the battle.

Destroyers *Yukikaze* and *Teruzuki* and cruiser *Nagara* engaged destroyer *Monssen* with gunfire after the American ship had launched an unsuccessful torpedo attack on *Hiei* and a gun attack on either *Ikazuchi* or *Inazuma*. The concerted and accurate Japanese gunfire soon brought *Monssen* to a halt. She sank with the loss of over half her crew.

The last ship to be reduced to scrap was the *Yudachi*, which had played such an important role in breaking up the American formation at the start of the battle. At about 1220hrs, she engaged *Sterett* with *Teruzuki*, disabled the American ship and killed 28 of her crew. At about 0226hrs, *Yudachi* was hit by a single torpedo and brought to a stop. Other ships damaged during the night included *Ikazuchi* which took at least six hits, knocking out her forward 5in. mount and killing 21. *Murasame* suffered damage to her forward boiler room. In exchange, the destroyer hit *Juneau* at 0204hrs with a single torpedo that put the cruiser out of action. On the American side, *Helena* suffered minor gunfire damage from three 5in. hits.

## The next morning

By daybreak, as the remaining operational ships from both sides were withdrawing, there were several cripples left afloat on Iron Bottom Sound. *Portland*, still circling as a result of rudder damage, sighted *Yudachi* at 12,500 yards and directed six 8in. salvoes in her direction at about 0430hrs. *Yudachi* rolled over and sank, but most of her crew was rescued by *Samidare*. At 0610hrs, *Hiei* spotted and engaged the crippled *Aaron Ward* at the range of about 26,000 yards. *Hiei* was able to straddle *Aaron Ward* on her third two-gun salvo, but the destroyer was not hit. The American ship was towed clear of the area after *Hiei* came under air attack and had to cease firing.

The remaining American ships still able to maneuver, the damaged cruisers *San Francisco*, *Helena* and *Juneau*, joined by the damaged *Sterett* and the unscathed *O'Bannon* and *Fletcher*, were heading out of the area when a Japanese submarine spotted the column. At 1101hrs, submarine *I-26* fired a spread of torpedoes at the withdrawing Americans. One torpedo hit *Juneau*, which caused a catastrophic magazine explosion sinking the 6,000-ton cruiser in seconds. Some 115 of her crew of almost 700 survived the explosion, but rescue efforts did not begin for days after the event. In the end, a total of ten crewmen survived her sinking. The total number of crewmen lost on *Juneau* was 683, a significant proportion of the 1,439 American sailors lost in this single action.

With the arrival of daylight, the fate of the damaged *Hiei* still hung in the balance. Five destroyers were ordered to provide protection to the crippled battleship and Japanese fighters were able to provide sporadic air cover throughout the day, but with the battleship unable to maneuver effectively and Henderson Field so close, there was little reason for the Japanese to be optimistic about her survival. Up until 0600hrs, the ship moved slowly to the north until flooding forced the crew to abandon the manual steering compartment. This resulted in a wide starboard turn, which kept *Hiei* circling in the same spot. The air attacks began at 0615hrs and 70 sorties were flown throughout the day against *Hiei*. Abe ordered *Kirishima* to return to the area at 0930hrs and take *Hiei* under tow. The scope of American air attacks forced him to abandon this scheme later, and, at 1020hrs, he ordered *Hiei*'s

# The First Naval Battle of Guadalcanal, November 13, 1942.
## The battle begins situation at 0150hrs

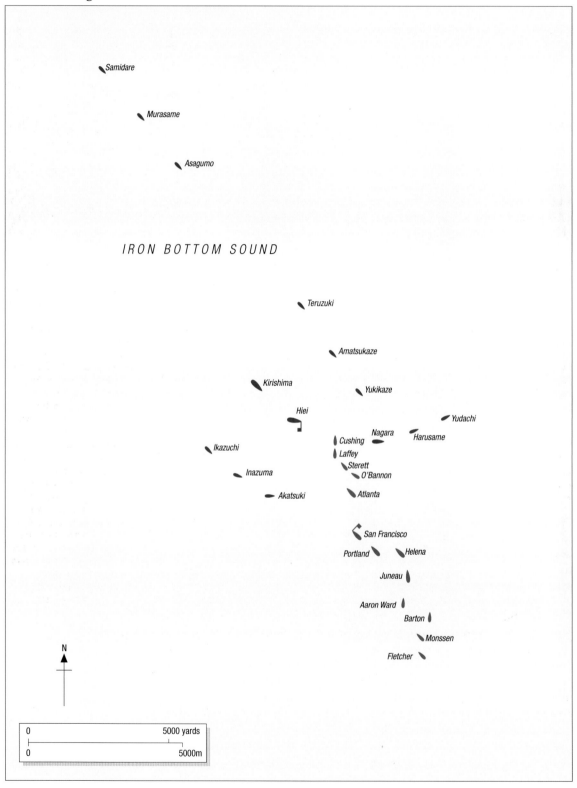

Samidare

Murasame

Asagumo

*IRON BOTTOM SOUND*

Teruzuki

Amatsukaze

Kirishima

Yukikaze

Hiei

Yudachi

Nagara

Cushing     Harusame

Ikazuchi

Laffey

Sterett

Inazuma     O'Bannon

Akatsuki     Atlanta

San Francisco

Portland     Helena

Juneau

Aaron Ward

Barton

Monssen

Fletcher

N

| 0 | 5000 yards |
|---|---|
| 0 | 5000m |

captain, Nishida Masao, to beach the battleship. Nishida refused this order since his ship was in no immediate danger of sinking. The first series of air attacks mounted by Marine dive-bombers, torpedo bombers from Henderson Field and carrier *Enterprise*, and even B-17s from Espiritu Santo were ineffective.

A torpedo plane attack just after noon placed two torpedo hits on *Hiei*, but the ship was still in no danger of sinking and the crew continued work on an emergency rudder. At 1235hrs, Abe ordered Nishida to get his crew off the ship during the next lull, but again he refused. The efforts of *Hiei*'s crew

seemed to be on the verge of success, with the fires being extinguished and progress made on pumping out the steering room. However, an attack at 1430hrs hit the battleship with two more torpedo hits on her starboard side. The ship developed a list and was down by the stern. All hope of repairing the steering was lost. An hour later, Abe ordered Nishida to abandon ship and this time the admiral remained firm in the face of protests. Despite the pounding she took, only 188 of *Hiei*'s crew were lost. Just as Abe was preparing to scuttle *Hiei* with destroyer torpedoes, orders were received from Yamamoto not to scuttle the ship so she could act as a decoy the next day to draw more American air attacks. Abe cleared the area at 1900hrs with his five destroyers, and when he returned at 0100 hrs, *Hiei* was gone, the first Japanese battleship to be lost during the war.

The Americans had paid a high price, but their sacrifice meant that the Japanese bombardment of the airfield was turned back. This allowed the aircraft from Henderson Field to savage the large convoy. American losses totaled two light cruisers and four destroyers sunk; both heavy cruisers sustained severe damage. Callaghan lost the opportunity to exploit his early detection of the Japanese, but following this indecision ordered an advance straight into the Japanese force where his lighter ships could do damage to the Japanese battleships. Though most of Abe's force was still combat ready after the battle, he had lost the action. *Hiei* was sunk, as well as destroyers *Akatsuki* and *Yudachi*. *Amatsukaze* and *Ikazuchi* were damaged and out of the fight, but Abe retained a second battleship, the redoubtable *Nagara* and seven combat-ready destroyers, most with their torpedoes still on board. His premature withdrawal cost the Japanese a chance for a greater tally of American ships.

### The battle builds

As bloody as the encounter of the night of November 12–13 was, it did not bring a decision. In response to the failure of his first bombardment attempt, Yamamoto changed the arrival of the 11-ship convoy to the 14th. Supporting the arrival of the convoy was still Yamamoto's primary objective and he ordered Kondo and Mikawa to renew efforts to bombard the airfield. The

*Aaron Ward* was a 2,060-ton Bristol-class destroyer commissioned in March 1942. This view of the ship was taken on August 17, 1942 as she was screening carrier *Wasp*. The ship is in the Measure 12 (modified) camouflage scheme. On top of the mainmast is the SC radar and the radar fire control director is evident above the bridge for the battery of four 5in. guns. *Aaron Ward* was present at the First Naval Battle of Guadalcanal and was in the thick of the action. She engaged a Japanese destroyer with gunfire, but was struck by nine shells and lost steering and finally power. Towed to Tulagi, she survived the battle. In April 1943, she was sunk by Japanese air attack off Guadalcanal and her wreck was discovered in 1994. (Naval History and Heritage Command, 80-G-12263)

Heavy cruiser *San Francisco* at Pearl Harbor on December 4, 1942, on her way to the United States for repairs after being damaged in the First Naval Battle of Guadalcanal. The ship was hit by an estimated 45 shells, causing extensive topside damage. (Naval History and Heritage Command, 80-G-21099)

first attempt to do so resulted in failure. On the night of November 13–14, two of Kondo's heavy cruisers, *Maya* and *Suzuya*, along with a light cruiser and four destroyers, entered Iron Bottom Sound and began to shell the airfield at 0130hrs on November 14. Though the force conducted the bombardment virtually unopposed and dispatched a total of 989 8in. shells at the target, the main airfield was missed. Only three aircraft were destroyed at the nearby auxiliary airfield, known as Fighter One. Mikawa had cautiously held back his two available heavy cruisers, *Chokai* and *Kinugasa*, from the bombardment in case the American fleet again intervened.

Now the Japanese failure to knock out the airfield paid immediate dividends for the Americans. First, search aircraft found the retreating Japanese cruiser force, sank *Kinugasa* and damaged *Maya* so badly she was forced to return to Japan. Meanwhile, the convoy had departed the anchorage at Shortland Island on the afternoon of November 13 under escort of Tanaka's 12 destroyers. Astoundingly, Yamamoto let the convoy advance toward the island before confirming that the airfield had been neutralized. Throughout the day on November 14, aviators from Henderson Field and carrier *Enterprise* made a supreme effort to destroy the incoming convoy. Six transports were sunk and another heavily damaged and forced to turn back. These attacks forced Tanaka behind schedule, and he considered temporarily suspending the operation, but was ordered by Yamamoto to continue south without regard to losses.

Once again, Yamamoto had failed to grasp the decisive moment. He still retained large forces under Kondo's command lingering north of Guadalcanal, including a second pair of fast battleships and several heavy cruisers. These were not committed in support of Abe's first attempt to neutralize the airfield, or on the following night. Now, after the convoy had already been largely destroyed, Kondo assembled another force to conduct a major effort. He gathered up the *Kirishima*, a couple of heavy cruisers and two destroyer squadrons and headed toward Guadalcanal with the intent of hitting the airfield during the early hours of November 15. This was far from a maximum effort since the fast battleships *Kongo* and *Haruna* were still not committed. Yamamoto did not intervene as Kondo put his plan together.

Halsey had much less to work with than Yamamoto, but was certainly more decisive. Halsey did not flinch from throwing all available surface forces into the fray. With Callaghan's task force shattered, Halsey had a single major asset remaining – his two fast battleships operating southeast of Guadalcanal with carrier *Enterprise*. After some debate on the wisdom of committing these heavy ships to the waters of Iron Bottom Sound, Halsey decided to send them north. They were too far away to intervene against Mikawa's cruiser bombardment on the night of November 13–14, but they arrived in the area ready to contest any Japanese operation the following night.

Halsey was taking a grave risk committing his last remaining surface assets. The task force he assembled, named Task Force 64, was a makeshift formation. Only four destroyers were available, and these had never worked together. The two battleships, *Washington* and *South Dakota*, had also never worked together and were not well trained for night combat. Halsey was exposing these ships, designed for long-range daytime gunnery duels with their Japanese counterparts, into confined waters at night where the torpedo threat was maximized. On the other hand, these were the most powerful ships in the United States Navy, and possibly in the world. Both possessed powerful and accurate 16in. naval rifles and the most modern radar-guided fire-control gunnery available.

## SECOND NAVAL BATTLE OF GUADALCANAL ORDER OF BATTLE

**UNITED STATES NAVY**

Task Force 64          Rear Admiral Willis Lee on *Washington*

    Battleships *South Dakota, Washington*

    Destroyers *Benham, Gwin, Preston, Walke*

**IMPERIAL JAPANESE NAVY**

Bombardment Group Vice          Admiral Kondo Nobutake on *Atago*

    Sentai 11

    Battleship *Kirishima*

    Sentai 4

    Heavy cruisers *Atago, Takao*

Screening Unit (Destroyer Squadron 10)          Rear Admiral Kimura Satsuma on *Nagara*

    Light cruiser *Nagara*

    Destroyer Division 9 *Asagumo*

    Destroyer Division 11 *Hatsuyuki, Shirayuki*

    Destroyer Division 61 *Teruzuki*

    Unassigned *Samidare, Inazuma*

Sweeping Unit (Destroyer Squadron 3)          Rear Admiral Hashimoto Shintaro on *Sendai*

    Light cruiser *Sendai*

    Destroyer Division 19 *Ayanami, Shikinami, Uranami*

Reinforcement Unit (Destroyer Squadron 2)          Rear Admiral Tanaka Razio on *Hayashio*

    Destroyer Division 15 *Oyashio, Kuroshio, Kagero*

    Destroyer Division 24 *Suzukaze, Kawakaze, Umikaze*

    Destroyer Division 31 *Makinami, Naganami, Takanami*

    Transports Kinugasa *Maru, Hirokawa Maru, Sangetsu Maru, Yamura Maru*

(The Reinforcement Unit was located to the east of the battle area; Tanaka dispatched *Oyashio* and *Kagero* on his own initiative to join the fight.)

# THE SECOND NAVAL BATTLE OF GUADALCANAL

Rear Admiral Willis Lee brought Task Force 64 into Iron Bottom Sound and moved west of Savo Island to intercept the Japanese force he knew was coming, based on a spotting report from an American submarine on the afternoon of November 14. Lee's battle plan reflected the improvised nature of his command. He pinned his hope on the big guns of his two battleships. He arranged his task force in a column with the destroyers close to the battleships.

*Kirishima* pictured in 1937 after her second major reconstruction. After conversion to fast battleships, the Kongo-class ships retained only battle cruiser level protection with an 8in. main armor belt. *Kirishima* was overwhelmed by American 16in. gunfire at the Second Naval Battle of Guadalcanal. (Yamato Museum, 071227)

Kondo had an inaccurate idea of what was waiting for him. Japanese reconnaissance aircraft had continually misidentified Task Force 64 as two cruisers and a number of destroyers. Kondo expected to have to fight his way into Iron Bottom Sound, but did not expect to face two battleships. Accordingly, his plan was for his two destroyer squadrons to neutralize the American force before bringing in his battleship and two heavy cruisers to crush the airfield.

From a position northwest of Cape Esperance, Lee brought his task force around Savo Island to the north and east, before entering Iron Bottom Sound. The nearest Japanese formation was the Sweeping Unit composed of Destroyer Squadron 3 with light cruiser *Sendai* and three destroyers. This force was entering Iron Bottom Sound by moving to the east of Savo Island. At 2313hrs on November 14, one of the Japanese destroyers spotted Lee's task force, providing yet another example of Japanese optics outperforming American electronics. One destroyer, *Ayanami*, was dispatched to scout the channel west of Savo Island and the rest of the force continued to scout the channel east of Savo Island.

The Japanese continued to track Lee's force as it began to head west after reaching a point southeast of Savo Island. They continued to identify the force as two cruisers and four destroyers. In response to this information, Kondo ordered the Screening Unit, with a light cruiser and four destroyers, to enter the channel south of Savo at 0015hrs and engage the Americans. He turned his heavy ships away to give the Screening Unit time to do its job.

Lee finally got a radar contact on the Sweeping Unit to his north at 18,000 yards at about 0001hrs. This was converted into a visual contact at 0012hrs, and two minutes later Lee ordered his battleships to engage the Japanese thinking that this was the Bombardment Group. At 0017hrs at a range of 18,500 yards, *Washington* opened the battle with a salvo of 16in.

# The Second Naval Battle of Guadalcanal

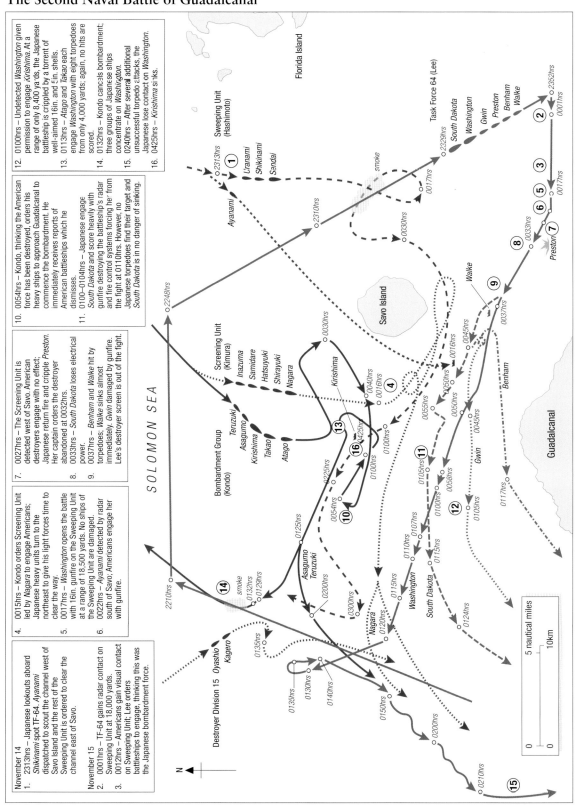

November 14
1. 2313hrs – Japanese lookouts aboard *Shikinami* spot TF-64. *Ayanami* dispatched to scout the channel west of Savo Island and the rest of the Sweeping Unit is ordered to clear the channel east of Savo.

November 15
2. 0001hrs – TF-64 gains radar contact on Sweeping Unit at 18,000 yards.
3. 0012hrs – Americans gain visual contact on Sweeping Unit; Lee orders battleships to engage, thinking this was the Japanese bombardment force.

4. 0015hrs – Kondo orders Screening Unit led by *Nagara* to engage Americans; Japanese heavy units turn to the northeast to give his light forces time to clear the way.
5. 0017hrs – *Washington* opens the battle with 16in. gunfire on the Sweeping Unit at a range of 18,500 yards. No ships of the Sweeping Unit are damaged.
6. 0022hrs – *Ayanami* detected by radar south of Savo; Americans engage her with gunfire.

7. 0027hrs – The Screening Unit is detected west of Savo. American destroyers engage with no effect; Japanese return fire and cripple *Preston*. Her captain orders the destroyer abandoned at 0032hrs.
8. 0033hrs – *South Dakota* loses electrical power.
9. 0037hrs – *Benham* and *Walke* hit by torpedoes; *Walke* sinks almost immediately. *Gwin* damaged by gunfire. Lee's destroyer screen is out of the fight.

10. 0054hrs – Kondo, thinking the American force has been destroyed, orders his heavy ships to approach Guadalcanal to commence the bombardment. He immediately receives reports of American battleships which he dismisses.
11. 0100–0104hrs – Japanese engage *South Dakota* and score heavily with gunfire destroying the battleship's radar and fire control systems forcing her from the fight at 0110hrs. However, no Japanese torpedoes find their target and *South Dakota* is in no danger of sinking.

12. 0100hrs – Undetected *Washington* given permission to engage *Kirishima*. At a range of only 8,400 yards, the Japanese battleship is crippled by a torrent of well-aimed 16in. and 5in. shells.
13. 0113hrs – *Atago* and *Takao* each engage *Washington* with eight torpedoes from only 4,000 yards; again, no hits are scored.
14. 0132hrs – Kondo cancels bombardment; three groups of Japanese ships concentrate on *Washington*.
15. 0240hrs – After several additional unsuccessful torpedo attacks, the Japanese lose contact on *Washington*.
16. 0425hrs – *Kirishima* sinks.

Ayanami was a unit in the second group of Special Type destroyer. She made numerous reinforcement runs to Guadalcanal before being assigned to the Japanese forces tasked to conduct a bombardment of Henderson Field on November 15. In this battle, she was handled aggressively by her skipper, but paid the price and was damaged by American gunfire before being scuttled. (Yamato Museum, 071982)

rounds, joined seconds later by *South Dakota*. The Japanese immediately turned away and made smoke. Despite several salvoes of 16in. and 5in. rounds from the battleships, no hits were scored against the Japanese. However, the admiral in charge of the Sweeping Unit continued to move to the east, effectively taking his three ships out of this phase of the battle.

The fourth ship of the Sweeping Unit was much more aggressive. After sweeping around to the west of Savo Island, *Ayanami* was south of Savo when she was detected by radar aboard destroyer *Walke*. Two American destroyers took the contact under fire commencing at 0022hrs and were joined by the 5in. secondary batteries aboard *Washington*.

Behind *Ayanami* by some 10,000 yards was the Screening Unit led by *Nagara*. This formation was spotted by destroyer *Preston* at 0027hrs, west of Savo. *Preston* and two other destroyers took this new threat under fire. The American gunfire was ineffective, but *Nagara*'s response was not. Several shells hit *Preston* and turned her into a flaming wreck. Her own torpedoes exploded at 0032hrs and her captain ordered the remaining crew to abandon ship.

Worse was yet to come. First *Ayanami*, and then the Screening Unit had launched torpedoes at the American destroyers. *Ayanami*'s eight torpedoes missed, but at 0037hrs, a torpedo hit *Benham* and blew her bow off. Another hit *Walke* forward and blew off her bow as well. *Gwin* had been hit earlier

Destroyer *Preston*, shown in this prewar view, was a Mahan-class unit. She fought at the battle of Santa Cruz and was then assigned to TF-64 for the Second Naval Battle of Guadalcanal. She was sunk with the loss of 117 of her crew. (Naval History and Heritage Command, NH 97937)

Walke, a Sims-class destroyer, was sunk at the Second Naval Battle of Guadalcanal by a Japanese torpedo. Eighty men from her crew were lost. She was selected to participate in the battle simply because she had the most fuel on board at the time Halsey dispatched TF-64 to Guadalcanal. This view, taken on August 24, 1942, shows the destroyer in her Measure 12 (modified) camouflage scheme at Mare Island Navy Yard before heading to the South Pacific. (Naval History and Heritage Command, NH 97911)

by at least two shells, which reduced her speed and made her incapable of further action. Lee's entire destroyer screen was now out of action. None of the American destroyers had even fired a single torpedo at the Japanese.

It was up to the battleships to repel the Japanese. Unfortunately for Lee, *South Dakota* began to experience a series of electrical failures, which essentially took her out of the battle. The shock of her gunfire tripped a circuit breaker, which led to the loss of electrical power on the entire ship. Without radar or power to service her guns, *South Dakota* was helpless for three key minutes. By the time power was restored, *South Dakota* had lost

Destroyer Benham was the lead ship of ten 1,500-ton destroyers ordered in 1936. They were armed with four 5in. guns and a heavy battery of 16 21in. torpedo tubes. This is Benham in February, 1942, off the Mare Island Navy Yard. Censors have deleted her radars. The ship was sunk in the Second Naval Battle of Guadalcanal but remarkably, none of her crew was lost. (Naval History and Heritage Command, NH 90936)

Battleship South Dakota was the lead ship of four 35,000-ton ships that entered service beginning in 1942. South Dakota reached the South Pacific in time to participate in the battle of Santa Cruz during which she claimed 26 Japanese aircraft shot down. She was paired with Washington to repel the Japanese in the Second Naval Battle of Guadalcanal, but was bedeviled by electrical problems, which left her blind for important parts of the battle. She was moderately damaged by Japanese shellfire in the battle. This view was taken in June 1943 after she had been repaired. (Naval History and Heritage Command, NH 97265)

## WASHINGTON ENGAGES KIRISHIMA (pp. 78–79)

On the night of November 14–15, 1942, both the Americans and Japanese committed battleships to the waters around Guadalcanal in what would be the first engagement of battleships during the Pacific War. In this confused action, the single Japanese battleship present, *Kirishima*, was among several Japanese ships to target the American battleship *South Dakota*. As *Kirishima* and several other Japanese ships focused on *South Dakota*, the second American battleship, *Washington*, targeted *Kirishima* from only 8,400 yards. At this pointblank range for 16in. guns, *Washington* engaged the relatively poorly protected Japanese battleship. This scene shows *Washington* (1) taking the surprised *Kirishima* (2) under fire with her 16in. main battery. The well-drilled gunnery team aboard *Washington* fired a total of 75 16in. shells at *Kirishima* and scored at least nine hits. Another 107 5in. shells were fired at the Japanese battleship with some 40 hits likely. With her main belt being limited to a maximum of 8in.,

*Kirishima* could not stand this kind of battering. Her forward turrets were knocked out in the first minutes of the action. By the time *Washington* ceased fire, *Kirishima* was on fire amidships and in her stern area. Her steering compartment was partially flooded and her rudders jammed. Underwater hits by the massive 16in. rounds had penetrated *Kirishima*'s armor and created a starboard list which the Japanese were unable to check. Though the fires were subsequently put out, *Kirishima* was beyond salvation with the increasing list and loss of propulsive power. In return, *Washington* was untouched by *Kirishima*'s sporadic and ineffective return fire. In the first battleship duel of the Pacific War, the Americans were the clear victors. *Washington*'s superb performance also brought to a close the last major Japanese effort to turn the tide of battle of the naval campaign for Guadalcanal.

contact with *Washington*, and was still focusing on engaging the *Sendai* located to her east.

On board *Washington*, her well-trained crew was already tracking a large target to the northwest. This was *Kirishima*. By 0040hrs, *Washington*'s gun crews were ready to engage this target, but since the location of *South Dakota* was uncertain, Lee did not permit *Washington* to open fire. Lee ordered *Benham* and *Gwin* to withdraw.

After a lull in the action, and after reports from *Ayanami* that the American force had been dealt with, at 0054hrs Kondo ordered his heavy ships to head to the southeast and approach Guadalcanal to conduct its bombardment mission. The Screening Unit then issued a report that it had sighted an American battleship in the path of the bombardment force. Kondo dismissed this report, but lookouts aboard *Atago* confirmed this startling information minutes later when they gained contact with *South Dakota*. Immediately, *Atago* put eight torpedoes in the water against this new threat and then used her searchlights to illuminate the battleship. The five ships of the bombardment force, battleship *Kirishima*, cruiser *Atago* and *Takao* and the two lead destroyers, *Asagumo* and *Teruzuki*, all engaged *South Dakota*. From 0100–0104hrs, the Japanese scored heavily against *South Dakota* with 18 8in., six 6in., and two smaller hits. *Kirishima* scored only a single 14in. hit and this succeeded only in blowing a hole in the main deck before being defeated by the armored barbette of the battleship's aft turret. The Japanese were confident that the damage inflicted was enough to sink the heavily armored battleship, but in reality she was in no danger of sinking since her watertight integrity was not threatened. *South Dakota* did take extensive topside damage, which destroyed her radar and fire control systems and left her out of the fight. Fortunately for the Americans, none of the eight torpedoes from *Atago* or four more from *Asagumo* found their mark.

While Japanese attentions were focused on *South Dakota*, the undetected *Washington* reentered the fight. At 0100hrs, Lee gave permission to engage *Kirishima* with *Washington*'s main battery. In seconds, 39 16in. shells were sent toward the unsuspecting *Kirishima* with dramatic results. From a range of only 8,400 yards, several of the 2,700lb shells hit *Kirishima*. *Washington* checked fire from 0002–0004hrs, and when she resumed, another 36 16in. rounds were directed at *Kirishima* with even

Kinugasa Maru was another of the four transports that reached Guadalcanal from the November convoy. The ship was beached on Tanaka's orders in an attempt to get her cargo ashore. It was later attacked and sunk by aircraft. (Naval History and Heritage Command, 80-G-K-1467-A)

more devastating effect. Both aft turrets were knocked out of action, fires grew amidships and aft, the rudder was jammed in a starboard turn and the steering room was partly flooded. Several underwater hits created a starboard list. *Washington*'s gun crews had shot very well, landing as many as nine 16in. and 40 5in. shells on the Japanese battleship. *Kirishima* had vainly tried to take her tormenter under fire, but all of her rounds fell short. In the first dreadnought duel of the Pacific War, the Americans clearly came out on top.

Lee was concerned about the location of *South Dakota*, and ordered another ceasefire. Unbeknownst to Lee, at 0110, *South Dakota*'s captain ordered his ship out of the fight. Without radios, he could not advise Lee of his decision. *South Dakota* had expended 115 16in. shells and 305 5in. with only a single possible hit on *Ayanami*. *Washington* was now left alone to contend with Kondo's still formidable force.

In the final phase of the battle, Kondo maneuvered his force to get a favorable torpedo solution on the *Washington*. Both sides were tracking the other, but neither knew it and neither wanted to open fire to reveal its position. At 0113hrs, *Atago* and *Takao* each unleashed eight torpedoes at

# The battle of Tassafaronga

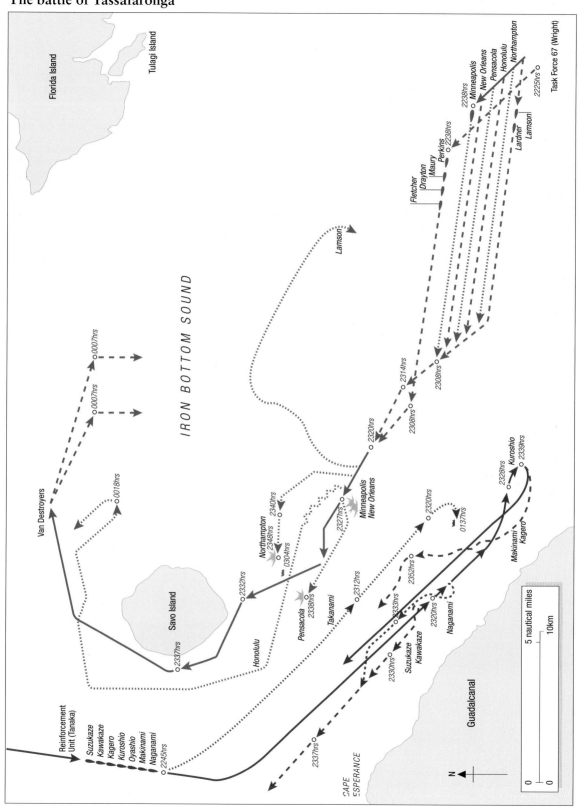

This is the aftermath of Abe's and Kondo's failure to bombard and neutralize Henderson Field. The beached and burned-out *Yamura Maru* is pictured in February, after the battle. She was one of only four Japanese transports to reach the island out of 11 ships; all but one were sunk or damaged by aircraft. (Naval History and Heritage Command, SC166450)

*Washington* from only 4,000 yards. Though the Japanese claimed hits, none was scored. At 0125hrs, Kondo ordered all his ships to concentrate on *Washington*. This was the period of greatest danger to Lee's flagship, as three groups of Japanese torpedo-armed ships gathered around him. Joining the fray were two destroyers from Tanaka's convoy, now located to the west. The Screening Unit had by this time reloaded its torpedo tubes and had also rejoined the fight. Tanaka's two destroyers and several ships of the Screening Unit launched torpedo attacks, but none found its target. Lee exited to the west of Guadalcanal and the Japanese lost contact at 0240hrs.

The cost of the battle was high for both sides. The Japanese were unable to save *Kirishima*. By 0349hrs most of the fires had been put out, but the ship was unnavigable since the steering compartment was flooded, and the attempts to steer with engines alone were unsuccessful *Nagara* briefly attempted to tow the battleship, but this too was unsuccessful. The flooding could not be stopped, and at 0425hrs the battleship rolled over to port and sank. A total of 212 men from her crew were lost, but three destroyers saved 1,128 men. *Ayanami*, damaged earlier in the action, also sank during the night with the loss of another 40 men. On top of the losses to Kondo's force, the last four transports from the convoy had been delayed in reaching Guadalcanal. Tanaka ordered them beached at 0400hrs and a hasty unloading of their supplies began. When morning came, American aircraft and a destroyer finished off the four transports and the hastily unloaded supplies sitting on the beach.

The cost to the victorious Americans was not insignificant, but certainly worth it. Destroyer *Benham* was scuttled after salvage attempts failed, joining the previously sunk *Preston* and *Walke*. *South Dakota* lived to fight another day, but 39 of her crew had been killed and another 59 wounded. American deaths in the battle totaled 242. *Washington*, almost miraculously, was untouched. Yamamoto's largest and last attempt to gain victory at Guadalcanal had been defeated.

# THE BATTLE OF TASSAFARONGA

The last naval battle of the Guadalcanal campaign was almost anticlimactic. With the destruction of their large convoy and the Americans willing to contest the waters off Guadalcanal at night, the Japanese were increasingly hard pressed to provide supplies and reinforcement for their garrison on the island. The latest method to reduce the vulnerability of destroyers engaged in Tokyo Express runs was to put supplies in watertight drums, which would be thrown off the destroyers' decks close to shore so that small boats from the island could tow them ashore.

Using this expedient, the Japanese planned five such runs, beginning on the night of November 29. The mission was entrusted to Rear Admiral Tanaka, the cool veteran of many Tokyo Express runs to the island. For this first mission, he had two destroyers assigned escort and six more acting as transports, with 200–240 drums aboard. The transport ships had their spare torpedoes removed to compensate for the topside weight of the supply drums.

The Americans were prepared to deny the Japanese the opportunity to land supplies to the beleaguered garrison. Halsey created a new surface force, Task Force 67, from newly arrived ships and several cruisers released from carrier screening duties. On November 28, Rear Admiral Carleton Wright was given command of the force, which totaled four heavy cruisers, one light cruiser and four destroyers. Wright inherited a battle plan that attempted to take advantage of the lessons learned from previous night battles. Among these was prominent use of the reliable and effective SG radar and using destroyers as scouts in advance of the cruisers where they would use their radar to launch a surprise torpedo attack.

Wright knew from multiple sources that the Tokyo Express would run on the night of November 29–30. He deployed four destroyers in the van with the SG-equipped *Fletcher* in the lead. Then came his five cruisers 4,000 yards behind. Behind them were two destroyers that Halsey had ordered to join Task Force 67 after escorting a convoy departing Guadalcanal.

Light cruiser *Honolulu* was the only American cruiser present at the battle of Tassafaronga that was not struck by Japanese torpedoes. This October 26, 1942, view shows the cruiser's heavy armament of 15 6in. guns in five triple turrets. (Naval History and Heritage Command, 19-N-36362)

FICIAL PHOTOGRAPH
T TO BE RELEASED
FOR PUBLICATION
'Y YARD MARE ISLAND. CALIF

RESTRICTED

## THE TORPEDOING OF *NORTHAMPTON* (pp. 86–87)

At the battle of Tassafaronga on November 30, 1942, a Japanese force of eight destroyers was engaged at night by a force of five American cruisers and six destroyers. For the loss of a single destroyer, the Japanese torpedoed four of the American cruisers. The last of these, *Northampton* (1), was hit by two Type 93 "Long Lance" torpedoes at 2348hrs on her port side (2). The resulting fires and flooding could not be controlled, and the ship sank at 0304hrs the following morning. This scene shows the instant when the two torpedoes hit the cruiser. The three other torpedoed cruisers survived, but did not return to service for between seven and 12 months. It was the greatest victory of the war for the IJN's destroyer force and was the result of well-trained crews using proven tactics to maximize the potential of the formidable Type 93 torpedo. Even this late in the campaign, American commanders did not understand the power of this weapon. By not maneuvering during the battle, Wright made his cruisers easy targets for the Japanese destroyers. The battle of Tassafaronga was the last time the Americans used major surface combatants in an attempt to disrupt Japanese resupply operations to Guadalcanal. Nevertheless, within some 10 weeks of this Japanese victory, the naval campaign for Guadalcanal was over with the result being a resounding Japanese defeat.

# THE BATTLE OF TASSAFARONGA ORDER OF BATTLE

## UNITED STATES NAVY

Task Force 67 Rear Admiral Carleton Wright in *Minneapolis*

Task Group 67.2.2

Heavy cruisers *Minneapolis, New Orleans, Pensacola*

Task Group 67.2.3

Heavy cruiser *Northampton*

Light cruiser *Honolulu*

Task Group 67.2.4

Destroyers *Fletcher, Drayton, Maury, Perkins*

Destroyer Division 9

Destroyers *Lamson, Lardner*

## IMPERIAL JAPANESE NAVY

Reinforcement Unit (Destroyer Squadron 2) Rear Admiral Tanaka Razio in *Naganami*

Screen (Destroyer Division 31)

Destroyers *Takanami, Naganami*

First Transportation Unit (Destroyer Division 15)

Destroyers *Kagero, Kuroshio, Makinami, Oyashio*

Second Transportation Unit (Destroyer Division 24)

Destroyers *Kawakaze, Suzukaze*

Tanaka entered Iron Bottom Sound to the south of Savo Island and approached the coast of Guadalcanal carefully. Destroyer *Takanami* was deployed 10 miles in advance as a scout. The rest of his force was arranged in a column. Between 2300hrs and midnight on November 29, the Japanese arrived off Cape Esperance and began moving toward their various supply drum drop points.

On this occasion, the American radar gave them the advantage. The first ship to gain contact was *Minneapolis*, when at 2306hrs her SG set reported ships to the west at 23,000 yards. Sharp-eyed lookouts on *Takanami* gained contact on the Americans at 2312hrs to the east. With this information, Tanaka was quick to react. Within minutes he had cancelled the resupply operation and prepared to fight.

What could have been a devastating first blow by Wright was wasted. When the commander of his lead destroyers asked permission for a beam torpedo attack against Tanaka's main body at 2316hrs, Wright refused until the target angle became acute. The American torpedo attack, launched at 2320 with a total of 15 torpedoes from three ships, was ineffective.

As the torpedoes were sent on their way, Wright unleashed a torrent of 8in. and 5in. gunfire against the Japanese. The object of most of this effort was *Takanami*, which, already burning from hits, attracted more attention. Before being disabled by an avalanche of over 400 5in., 6in. and 8in. rounds, she fired her full load of eight Type 93 torpedoes. Even though she was a flaming wreck when her torpedoes struck, this broadside proved effective. Two torpedoes struck *Minneapolis* at 2327hrs, one forward and one amidships. Another torpedo hit the next cruiser in line, *New Orleans*. The power of the

Heavy cruiser *Minneapolis* at Tulagi on December 1, after being torpedoed at the battle of Tassafaronga the previous day. The wreckage of her bow was cut away and a new temporary bow built to allow her to return to the United States for repairs. *Minneapolis* did not return to service until October 1943. (Naval History and Heritage Command, 80-G-211215)

Heavy cruiser *New Orleans* lies camouflaged at Tulagi after losing her bow in the battle of Tassafaronga. The cruiser was able to return to the United States for repairs but did not return to service until September 1943. Though Tulagi was an austere base, during the campaign it did provide temporary sanctuary for several damaged ships, which otherwise would have been lost. In contrast, any Japanese ship damaged in Iron Bottom Sound and unable to move away was lost when daylight commenced and American aircraft intervened. (Naval History and Heritage Command, 80-G-216014)

torpedo, combined with the contents of one of the forward magazines, broke the bow off as far back as the second 8in. turret.

The next cruiser in line was *Pensacola*, which now became an attractive target as she passed by the burning wrecks of the two torpedoed cruisers. Several Japanese destroyers took the opportunity to unleash their weapons at *Pensacola*. Of the 26 torpedoes launched by *Kawakaze*, *Naganami*, *Kuroshio* and *Oyashio*, one hit her amidships at 2338hrs and immediately disabled her. Ten minutes later, two additional torpedoes, possibly from this same salvo, hit *Northampton* as she approached Savo Island. These caused massive flooding and fires, and the cruiser sank at 0304hrs.

Many American observers commented upon the effectiveness of the radar-controlled gunnery, which seemed to hit and sink their targets. In fact, with the exception of the unfortunate *Takanami*, the only other success was slight damage to *Naganami*. By any means, it was difficult to hit a maneuvering destroyer at full speed, and on this occasion the Americans were forced to rely primarily on radar guidance; and the already-discussed problem of chasing shell splashes probably accounts for the ineffectiveness of the volumes of gunnery. An indication of the general confusion present was shown by the fact that the two American destroyers in the rear of the formation were both engaged by cruiser gunnery, though neither suffered damage. Wright claimed that 17 Japanese ships were present and that nine were sunk.

This last action of the campaign confirmed that the IJN retained its edge in night combat. Tanaka had scored a brilliant victory though he was surprised and his ships were encumbered by cargo on their decks. His well-drilled crews, using the incomparable Type 93 torpedo, scored a signal victory. The only ship lost, *Takanami*, suffered 211 dead and another 26 captured. Only 33 reached shore and survived.

Wright had assisted Tanaka's quick-response torpedo attacks by maintaining a steady course through much of the action, making his ships excellent targets. Even at this late stage in the campaign, the Americans had no idea of the true capabilities of the Type 93. In addition to the *Northampton*, which was sunk with the loss of 50 men, the other three cruisers' torpedoes were out of the war for extended periods. *New Orleans* would not return for nine months, and she had lost 183 men. *Minneapolis* suffered 37 men dead and was out for 10 months. *Pensacola* would not return to action for an entire year, and 125 men of her crew would never return.

Heavy cruiser *Pensacola* at Espiritu Santo on December 17, 1942. The cruiser is alongside repair ship *Vestal* to conduct temporary repairs of damage received on November 30 during the battle of Tassafaronga. Note the patch on the hull aft and extensive fire damage. *Pensacola* did not return to service until late 1943. (Naval History and Heritage Command, 80-G-33862)

# THE AFTERMATH

## THE END OF THE CAMPAIGN

Another result of the battle of Tassafaronga was that Halsey decided to stop using destroyers and cruisers to contest Japanese transport missions to Guadalcanal. For the remainder of the campaign, only PT boats were used against the Japanese. The Japanese tactics of using supply drums was a miserable failure, with only a small fraction of the drums dropped off during the next three destroyer missions reaching shore. On December 11, PT boats scored a rare success by torpedoing the large destroyer *Teruzuki*, which Tanaka was using as his flagship. The fires could not be contained, and when they reached the depth charges, the ship blew up. Tanaka and all but nine of the crew were saved, but this event underscored the high cost of maintaining the tenuous lifeline to Guadalcanal. It was the last time the IJN entered the waters off Guadalcanal in 1942.

By this time, Imperial General Headquarters was already laying the groundwork for orders to abandon Guadalcanal. The campaign had not only derailed the New Guinea campaign, which was held as a higher priority than Guadalcanal, but Japan's logistical capabilities were proving inadequate to supporting efforts in the South Pacific. The Navy Section at Imperial Headquarters made it clear that continued losses would make it impossible for the Navy to win a future decisive battle, demonstrating their inability to see what had been unfolding for the last five months. Bowing to the inevitable since both the Army and the Navy had lost confidence in their ability to continue the campaign, Imperial General Headquarters agreed to a withdrawal on December 26. The Emperor approved this new strategy on December 31. Now it was up to the IJN to start the withdrawal of the remaining garrison, which was planned to begin in late January.

Japanese preparations for the withdrawal were mistaken by the Americans for preparations for a renewed offensive. To execute the evacuation, the IJN used all available resources and brought additional air reinforcements to cover the withdrawal. Despite predictions by many that the operations would result in heavy losses to the Navy's dwindling numbers of destroyers, the operation was well-executed and proved to be a total success. The obvious question is why such resources were not devoted to supply and reinforcement missions. On three nights, February 1, 4 and 7, a total of 58 destroyers were committed to take off the pathetic, emaciated survivors of 17th Army.

A total of 10,652 men were saved in this fashion, and only a single destroyer was lost, probably to mines. With the cessation of organized resistance on February 9, the campaign came to a close.

The campaign for Guadalcanal lasted six months. During this time, five major naval battles were fought between surface units at night and two major carrier battles were recorded. The results of these actions, in addition to the smaller encounters, which routinely occurred during this struggle between surface units, submarines and aircraft, were major losses for both sides. United States Navy losses totaled 25 major surface units while the IJN lost another 18. These totals do not include the many ships damaged. The ferocity of the combat is shown by the fact that all 11 of the American heavy cruisers comitted to surface combat were sunk or damaged by the end of the campaign. The exact nature of these losses is given in the table below. These totals do not include losses in submarines and transports, which ran heavily against the Japanese.

**Naval losses during the Guadalcanal campaign**

|  | Carriers (heavy/light) | Battleships | Cruisers (heavy/light) | Destroyers |
|---|---|---|---|---|
| USN | 2/0 | 0 | 6*/2 | 15 |
| IJN | 0/1 | 2 | 3/1 | 11 |

*Includes heavy cruiser *Australia*

Once the enormity of Japan's naval losses are considered, and added to the loss of some 1,100 naval aircraft from both combat and operational causes and most of their highly-trained crews, the campaign can only be considered a disaster for the Japanese. Guadalcanal shapes up much more convincingly as the single most decisive battle in the Pacific War. Whereas Midway stopped Japanese expansion in the Central Pacific, the campaign for Guadalcanal stopped the threat to Australia and the South Pacific lifelines to Australia. The Japanese attempted to stop the first American counterattack against their perimeter, and, despite committing the bulk of the IJN, they failed. With the flood of new American naval and air units reaching the theater, the Japanese could not risk another major attempt to disrupt the American advance until June 1944. At that point, the Americans threatened Japan's inner defenses and forced the Japanese into a major battle. Again, the Japanese suffered defeat.

The American offensive had been mounted sooner than the Japanese had expected, and as a result gained both tactical and strategic surprise. The Japanese, under Yamamoto's direction, were slow to respond and Yamamoto never realized that this was his long-desired decisive battle against the US Navy. He let this opportunity escape his grasp, and as a result the available Allied strength proved just sufficient to defeat every Japanese attempt to gain victory. On the other hand, Halsey and Turner exhibited a clarity of purpose and a ruthlessness unmatched by the Japanese. In the end, their aggressiveness provided the measure of victory.

Looking at the surface battles covered in this book, the picture is also mixed. The Japanese were the undoubted victors of the first and last major naval battles of the campaign, though on both occasions they were heavily outnumbered. Savo Island set the tone for much of the campaign as the Japanese demonstrated their superior nightfighting tactics and equipment.

However, despite the signal victory over the unprepared Allied surface forces covering the initial landing, the battle represented a massive lost opportunity for the Japanese. The final battle of the campaign in late November at Tassafaronga was impressive, but had come too late to have any more than tactical significance.

The United States Navy possessed a revolutionary capability in radar. Even with this, only two battles during the campaign were clear American victories. In both of these, radar played an important, if not decisive role. At Cape Esperance, radar allowed Scott to surprise the Japanese. Just as Japanese surprise led to Allied disaster at Savo Island, the advantage gained by radar at Cape Esperance proved decisive. At the Second Naval Battle of Guadalcanal, Halsey broke all the rules by committing his only battleships in torpedo-infested waters. The gamble paid off because of the coolness and luck of Lee and the excellence of *Washington*'s radar-controlled 16in. guns.

Like no other battle, the First Naval Battle of Guadalcanal fought on November 13 typified the intense struggle between the American and Japanese. This slugfest resulted in heavy losses on both sides, but the American losses, while heavier, served a greater purpose as they protected the airfield at the most crucial point in the campaign. The following day, aircraft from Henderson Field swung the entire campaign in the Americans' favor when they sank the first Japanese battleship of the war and then devastated the large convoy of transports headed for the island. In this battle, as well as the entire campaign, it is difficult to deny that the Japanese performed better where surface battles were concerned. Surface actions resulted in 15 American and Australian ships being sunk – five heavy cruisers, one light cruiser and nine destroyers. In contrast only eight Japanese ships were lost to surface action – one battleship, one heavy cruiser and six destroyers. *Hiei* would have survived her wounds from November 13, but was finished off by aircraft from Henderson Field. In the final analysis, it was the application of American airpower that supplied the margin of victory.

*Chicago* was the first American heavy cruiser damaged in the campaign; in January 1943, she was the last of six heavy cruisers to be sunk in the campaign during the battle of Rennell Island. This is *Chicago* on January 30, down by the stern after taking several aircraft torpedoes. (Naval History and Heritage Command, 80-G-38823)

# BIBLIOGRAPHY

Crenshaw, Russell, *The Battle of Tassafaronga*, Nautical and Aviation Publishing Company of America, Baltimore (1995)

Cook, Charles, *The Battle of Cape Esperance*, Naval Institute Press, Annapolis (1992)

Dull, Paul S., *A Battle History of the Imperial Japanese Navy 1941–45*, Naval Institute Press, Annapolis (1978)

Frank, Richard B., *Guadalcanal*, Random House, New York (1990)

Fuller, Richard, *Japanese Admirals 1926–1945*, Schiffer, Atglen (2011)

Grace, James W., *The Naval Battle of Guadalcanal*, Naval Institute Press, Annapolis (1999)

Hone, Trent, "'Give Them Hell!': The US Navy's Night Combat Doctrine and the Campaign f or Guadalcanal" in *War in History* (2006), Vol. 13 No. 2

Hara, Tameichi, *Japanese Destroyer Captain*, Naval Institute Press, Annapolis n.d.

Hornfischer, James D., *Neptune's Inferno*, Bantam Books (2011)

Loxton, Bruce and Coulthard-Clark, *The Shame of Savo*, Naval Institute Press, Annapolis (1994)

Lundstrom, John B., *The First Team and the Guadalcanal Campaign*, Naval Institute Press, Annapolis (1994)

——, *Black Shoe Carrier Admiral*, Naval Institute Press, Annapolis (2006)

Morison, Samuel Eliot, *The Struggle for Guadalcanal* (*Volume V of The History of United States Naval Operations in World War II*), Little, Brown and Company, Boston (1975)

Newcomb, Richard F., *The Battle of Savo Island*, Holt, Rinehart and Winston, New York (1981)

O'Hara, Vincent P., *The U.S. Navy Against the Axis*, Naval Institute Press, Annapolis (2007)

Ohmae, Toshikazu, "The Battle of Savo Island" in *The Japanese Navy in World War II*, David C. Evans (ed), Naval Institute Press, Annapolis (2006)

Reardon, Jeff, "Breaking the U.S. Navy's 'Gun Club' Mentality in the South Pacific" in *The Journal of Military History* 75 (April 2011)

Reynolds, Clark G., *Famous American Admirals*, Van Nostrand-Reinhold Company, New York (1978)

Tanaka, Razio, "The Struggle for Guadalcanal" in *The Japanese Navy in World War II*, David C. Evans (ed), Naval Institute Press: Annapolis, Maryland, 2006

Warner, Denis and Peggy, *Disaster in the Pacific*, Naval Institute Press, Annapolis (1992)

www.combinedfleet.com

The following Osprey titles are also useful for additional background to the battles:

Stille, Mark, New Vanguard 146: *Imperial Japanese Navy Battleships 1941–45*, Osprey Publishing Ltd, Oxford (2008)

——, Campaign 214: *The Coral Sea 1942*, Osprey Publishing Ltd, Oxford (2009)

——, Duel 22: *USN Cruiser vs. IJN Cruiser*, Osprey Publishing Ltd: Oxford (2009)

——, Campaign 226: *Midway 1942*, Osprey Publishing Ltd, Oxford (2010)

——, New Vanguard 176: *Imperial Japanese Navy Heavy Cruisers 1941–45*, Osprey Publishing Ltd, Oxford (2011)

——, New Vanguard 187: *Imperial Japanese Navy Light Cruisers 1941–45*, Osprey Publishing Ltd, Oxford (2011)

——, Command 26: *Yamamoto Isoroku*, Osprey Publishing Ltd, Oxford (2012)

——, Duel xx: *USN Destroyer vs. IJN Destroyer*, Osprey Publishing Ltd: Oxford (2013)

# INDEX

Note: Page references in **bold** refer to photographs, diagrams and captions.